CREEP

Before you start to read this book, take this moment to think about making a donation to punctum books, an independent non-profit press,

@ https://punctumbooks.com/support/

If you're reading the e-book, you can click on the image below to go directly to our donations site. Any amount, no matter the size, is appreciated and will help us to keep our ship of fools afloat. Contributions from dedicated readers will also help us to keep our commons open and to cultivate new work that can't find a welcoming port elsewhere. Our adventure is not possible without your support.

Vive la open-access.

Fig. 1. Hieronymus Bosch, *Ship of Fools* (1490–1500)

First published in 2017 by punctum books, Earth, Milky Way.
https://punctumbooks.com

ISBN-13: 978-1-947447-10-3 (print)
ISBN-13: 978-1-947447-10-3 (ePDF)

LCCN: 2017950838
Library of Congress Cataloging Data is available from the Library of Congress

Copy editing: Mariana Flores Duron Lizaola
Book design: Mariana Flores Duron Lizaola & Vincent W.J. van Gerven Oei
Cover image: Pere Borrell del Caso, *Escaping Criticism* (1874). Courtesy of Banco de España, Madrid.

HIC SVNT MONSTRA

Jonathan Alexander

Creep

A Life · A Theory · An Apology

For Wayne Koestenbaum, whom I've never met.

Contents

Acknowledgments

Who wants to be thanked for such a book? Perhaps it's creepy to insist on expressing gratitude, but here goes. For support, for being there, for working with me on either this or an adjacent project, for seeming to like me despite my creepiness: Karen Yescavage, David J. Lumb, Jon Hughes, Jami Bartlett, Jackie Rhodes, David Wallace, Martha Marinara, Michael Szalay, Andrea Henderson, Susan C. Jarratt, Nasrin Rahimieh, George Lang, and Sue Cross. Antoinette LaFarge provided superb drawings to illustrate some of my creepier points. Jon Hughes (photopresse) took the fabulous photograph of me on the devastated beach of Bay St. Louis, Mississippi. And, as always, Mack McCoy has been my constant companion, even when I've kept him in the dark about my writing. Sorry, Mack, and thanks for just being you.

I also thank Ron Carlson for reading and commenting on a full draft of the manuscript. Special thanks to Tom Lutz, who first published bits and pieces of this work in the *Los Angeles Review of Books,* one of my first — and best — homes for this kind of writing. Thanks too to the editors at Computers and Composition Digital Press for allowing me to recast some of my writing about Glen from *Techne: Queer Meditations on Writing the Self.* Thanks also to Mark West, who solicited some writing about growing up gay in the south, and the editors of *Southern Quarterly* for first publishing some of the passages about my early love affair with the Baptist hymnal in the essay "Outside Within: Growing Up Gay in the South" (vol. 54, no. 3/4). And, most assuredly, I thank Eileen Joy who welcomed this project with open arms and generous spirit, and Vincent W.J. van Gerven Oei who shepherded me graciously through the production process.

In so many ways, this book owes its largest debt to Michelle Latiolais, colleague and friend, who not only introduced me to the work of Maggie Nelson, which inspired me in many ways, but who then read and commented on the full manuscript, pointing out where my creepiness strayed into the downright uncool. In deepest gratitude, thank you, Michelle, and I hope it's not insulting to have your name so closely associated with this little project.

Introduction

I'm sitting in a hipster coffee shop — excuse me, coffee *lab* — not far from my home in Irvine, California. Like most days, the sun is peeking over the mountains through some morning ocean fog, and the traffic has already started to accumulate. For over a year now, I've gotten up early to head with my laptop and fetch an overpriced cup of coffee, offering myself the best hours of the day for writing. This coffee shop is one of the ones I frequent. The coffee is actually very good, and the baristas, all young folk with their careful haircuts and corded pants, just a touch of blocky plaid creating contrast with the sculpted curves of facial hair, have gotten to know me. Somewhat. At first, they seemed hesitant. I'm not the usual clientele. I'm nearly 50, and while I can dress well, I have often shown up here in my sweatpants and a t-shirt, baseball cap not quite keeping the stray curls of my long forehead hair in check. I must look unkempt, at best, on those days. But the coffee jockeys have become accustomed to me, and some familiarity has lessened their intuitive contempt.

I take my $4 cup of coffee — something called Alchemistic, which is, some mornings, stunningly good: the hot water sifted in some magical way through the specialty coffee in a fancy machine made by a company called Alphadominche, that only makes these machines for upscale coffee shops—and head around the corner of the coffee bar to write. It's just a little after 7 a.m., and the place will slowly fill up within the hour. No one will talk to me — probably a combination of my sitting here typing on this machine but also my obvious misplacement. *Which one of these is not like the other?* The lesson is well ingrained. A young guy, immaculately coiffed, with what I call precision hair, can flirt with the baristas, male or female, and keep coming back day after day, a welcome sight. He's a good-looking dude, and another regular like me, someone I sometimes see pulling up to the shop in his sporty little blue Mini Cooper. I have neither his youth nor good looks, the winning combination. But I have come to know my place as I sit here typing away. I do try at times to be friendly, to approach the generational barrier, to peek at what's on the other side. It's not easy, though. I once asked to see a young woman's hand tattoo as she set a cup of coffee down in front of me, and she looked at me as though I'd slapped her. She showed me, but it was… weird. I try to remember that this is the generation of "trigger warnings," and it's often a hair trigger, easily set off. My showing up here isn't part of their curated world. I'm the oddball out, as we used to say.

Indeed, "odd" doesn't capture it. I begin to worry that my presence here is… *creepy*. These kids want to serve one another, be seen with one another, not be on display for me. I'm intruding. And in forcing them to accommodate themselves to me, I'm acting a bit strange — and I know it. But maybe I'm overstating the case? Maybe I'm just feeling my years as never before. After all, I'm easily double the age of most people here, sitting with my laptop, pounding away at the keyboard, letting loose an unexpected chortle as I write my way into some insight that is probably only fascinating to me. They might think I'm autistic. Or worse, lonely. But I return, perhaps masochistically, to buy the expensive coffee in this place I don't quite fit in.

I take out my phone to check text messages. Often the usual: various friends pinging me, one in particular from Ohio, a former colleague and dearly loved soul who, just a few years older than I, has been diagnosed with MS. We enjoy quick regular chats, often daily, continuing to be a part of each other's lives if only for moments at a time. She can't walk anymore, can't work, and can barely read, so little messages from two thousand miles away help keep her at least somewhat connected to the world.

Frankly they do the same for me. She's been such a part of my life the past twenty years.

Then I look through my photos. I'm always taking shots of things that interest me. One of the baristas, one I'm a little bit attracted to, comes around and bends down right in front of me, scouting out something beneath the counter. I hear the fumbling as I watch his ass bob up and down with the search. It's so quick I barely notice that I'm snapping a pic of his behind. And again. The phone doesn't make a sound. He finds what he's looking for and walks away, but not before looking over his shoulder to ask me if the Alchemistic is okay. Yes, yes it is, thank you. And I realize, oh fuck: I'm a total fucking creep.

I don't delete the picture.

This is a book about being creepy. It's part memoir, part analysis, and part explanation. It's not a defense. I'm creepy at times, no doubt. And if I conclude this book with an apology, I mean it in the old sense of *apologia,* that old genre somewhere between an impassioned defense (think Socrates, that early Athenian creep accused of corrupting youth and consequently sentenced to death) and a recognition of having erred, if defiantly, because I think my creepiness needs, if not defense, at least some accounting that invites you to understand how I became creepy, how I understand myself as creepy, why others might think so, and why, ultimately, I make peace with my own creepiness. Or at least try to. This writing, like most writing, is the making peace. I worry, like any writer, that perhaps what I'm really doing though is just making pieces — pieces that won't cohere. But I can't worry too much about that at this point. I have needed to let the writing, in a word, creep toward meaningfulness.

Like many of us, in fact, especially if you are reading this book, you might be wondering if you are a creep, or perhaps you've creeped yourself out at times, or more likely been creeped on by someone else. Creepiness fascinates, perhaps in part because we've all had the experience of being creeped on, while also worrying over our own potential for creepiness.

Indeed, "creep" as a designation, a category, suffers from some capacious indeterminacy. We know it when we see it. Or do we? Is creep a verb or a noun, an activity anyone is subject to engaging in periodically, or is it a particular identity accruing to individuals displaying a set of habits or even just occupying a way of being in the world that is unsettling? We creep on people, we can be creeped out, and sometimes folks are just plain creepy.

To get a sense of the range of creepiness, I set up a Google alert on the word "creep" and have promptly received, every day for over a year, a digest of roughly 8–10 articles *per day* that come out using the word. Often the word just designates a slow change, such as interest rates creeping up, or the earlier and earlier selling of Christmas items and the playing of holiday music well before Thanksgiving. But even such usage signals danger or at least the untoward, something amiss, out of place. Something *wrong*.

Adam Gopnik, writing for *The New Yorker*, uses the word prominently in the title of an article, "Donald Trump: Narcissist, Creep, Loser," to lambast the "brutal, vile, woman-despising, sexually predatory vulgarian" during the billionaire's campaign for the presidency. Gopnik never defines creep precisely, but we get a sense that creepiness is characterized by a combination of self-absorption and the pathetic, and he's at pains to describe the man who would soon be elected president as both vulnerable and dangerous, "a loser, struggling to impress a very insignificant new acquaintance with pitiful boasts about his masculinity," but a loser who may ultimately be driven to "unleash his demons" in an assault on his enemies and those who reject him.[1] Creep is a word that has attached readily to Trump, even after the election. Using the word as an adjective this time, the SocialistWorker.org eagerly announced that the "Trump creep show gets ready for the big stage," as the president-elect selected a variety of conservative thinkers and politicians, some with potential ties to white nationalism, to fill federal slots.[2] Creeps indeed. But it's Gopnik's blending of both internal and external damage — the botched individual who could potentially hurt others — that captures, if not a precise diagnosis of creepiness, at least a deeply felt sense of what being creepy is — the threat we respond to when calling someone a creep.

Once you start looking, creepiness is everywhere, often readily on display to castigate behavior we find objectionable, or worse. Many of us get a real dose of creepiness watching shows such as "To Catch a Predator," which focuses each episode on a guy (almost always a guy) lured to a child's home with the promise of illicit activity, usually of a sexual nature. The "child," of course, is never a child, but the predators who follow up their online exchanges by actually showing up for a rendezvous are all real people who are then confronted not with the object of their perverse desires but a reporter who generally startles them into confessing that they are indeed perverts. Most often the encounter ends with an arrest.

Surely such predators are creeps, and shows such as "To Catch a Predator" have spawned a variety of imitators, including some vigilante groups in Canada and the UK who pretend to be children, lure pervs into meeting up, and then either beat the crap out of them, call the cops, or both. The proliferation of such creep catching is actually bemoaned at times by various offi-

1 Adam Gopnik, "Donald Trump: Narcissist, Creep, Loser," *The New Yorker,* October 9, 2016, http://www.newyorker.com/news/news-desk/donald-trump-narcissist-creep-loser.

2 Eric Ruder, "Trump Creep Show Gets Ready for the Big Stage," *Socialist-Worker.org,* November 17, 2016, https://socialistworker.org/2016/11/17/trump-creep-show-ready-for-the-big-stage.

cial police organizations, who complain that the hobbyist creep catchers often interfere with formal investigations, particularly when the lay and official entities are targeting the same creeps.

I will admit, even at the price of seeming creepy, that I always feel just a tiny bit creeped out by the whole creep catching phenomenon. Yes, absolutely—child molestation is a terrible crime. As someone who was sexually abused as a child, I can attest to the lasting damage that such assault leaves on the psyches, and often the bodies, particularly in terms of body image, on the abused. Sexual predators *are* creeps. But I think that it's also pretty creepy to invite viewers to tune into the vicarious thrill of luring someone, even a predator, into a trap, springing it, watching them squirm, and then delighting in justice served. The difference, of course, is that the latter form of creepiness is sanctioned, so it rarely feels creepy.

In so many ways, we have become acculturated to a variety of different kinds of "creeping." Multiple news reports about Facebook use the word "creep" to describe, for instance, the "[X Number of] Things Facebook Is Doing that Will Creep You Out" or how "Facebook Live Video Map Lets Users Creep People Around the World in Real Time." More alarmingly, governmental agencies are in on the ubiquitous information gathering and storage game, with reports steadily coming out warning us that if we "think the US monitors your data too closely" then "China will really creep you out."[3] While variations on the word "creep" are deployed here to be alarming, I think it's probably

3 For more information, see Soorraj Shah's article, "5 things Facebook Is Doing That Will Creep You Out," *The Inquirer,* June 26, 2016, http://www.theinquirer.net/inquirer/feature/2463257/5-things-facebook-is-doing-that-will-creep-you-out; Susmita Baral, "Facebook Live Video Map Lets Users Creep On People Around The World In Real Time," *iDigital Times,* May 23, 2016, http://www.idigitaltimes.com/facebook-live-video-map-lets-users-creep-people-around-world-real-time-535885; and a similar article, "Trump creep show gets ready for the big stage," *Dallas News,* November 17, 2016, http://www.dallasnews.com/business/technology/headlines/20160628-think-the-u.s.-monitors-your-data-too-closely-china-will-really-creep-you-out.ece.

creepier that more and more people are just accepting that such monitoring is increasingly *normal.* Psychologists even tell us that younger generations grow up expecting less privacy then preceding generations, so what was once considered creepy can change over time.

Some folks even seem to perform creepiness professionally. Milo Yiannopoulos is one such professional creep who, now banned forever from Twitter, has spent much of his young adulthood trolling progressives and leftists online, making fun of people who disagree with him, and oddly flaunting his own gayness in the service of promoting the alt-right agenda. A writer for Breitbart, he's something of a mess: cute and snide, he came to national attention by mocking a black star of the female-cast reboot of *Ghostbusters* as a man in drag, campaigning as one of the "Gays for Trump," and decidedly being on the wrong side of Gamergate, identifying women who complain about sexism in video games as the worst kinds of feminists. He seems to be particularly vexed by transgender folks: "You really expect me to believe that I shouldn't laugh about trannies? It's hilarious. Like, dude thinks he's a woman?"[4]

I first became aware of Milo when I ran into a poorly made poster on my campus announcing his upcoming event, sponsored by the Campus Republicans and the Campus Libertarians. The eye-catching slogan, intentionally provocative, asked, "Who are we to let such dangerous faggotry go unpunished?" Apparently, this question was just attention-getting, not a call to action, but it certainly got *my* attention, as well as that of on campus; protests against Milo's visit quickly organized. My *personal* reaction to the sign was complex. At first, I was shocked, even amazed that, in a place like sunny California, we could still find such

4 For an insightful analysis of Milo, see this article: Chadwick Moore, "Send In the Clown: Internet Supervillain Milo Doesn't Care That You Hate Him," *Out,* September 21, 2016, http://www.out.com/out-exclusives/2016/9/21/send-clown-internet-supervillain-milo-doesnt-care-you-hate-him.

hateful speech. But I soon realized that this was just a bit of unfortunate provocation, even as I still worried that younger queer folk would—justifiably—find themselves not just insulted but even threatened by such "advertisement." Indeed, what's most obnoxious about the persona Milo performs publicly is his seeming failure of imaginative sympathy, an unwillingness to put himself sufficiently in someone else's shoes to understand how they might feel. Such a stance, often resulting in the imposition of one's thoughts and feelings on another, can certainly come across as creepy. But then again, perhaps Milo wouldn't mind being called a creep. It's a strategy, a pose, a performance.

And I get that. We all perform at times. And I'll even admit to finding Milo's outrageousness a little attractive, even if his tactics and messages are far more often than not, reprehensible. But he's cute enough, making his shenanigans worth a spanking. Indeed, I'd like to spank this young man. He deserves it. As soon as I say such a thing, though, I wonder: who's the creep now?

To be sure, creepiness is a moving target, subject to differing and varying norms of behavior that change over time. That doesn't mean that social scientists don't at times try to isolate what creepiness is. One study that surveyed over a thousand participants, apparently from an international pool of folks averaging 29 years of age, attempted to determine what kinds of things — or people — participants found creepy. The surveyors concluded, as an article appearing in *Slate* summarizes, that "a person's 'creepiness detector' pings when she encounters something unpredictable or outside the norm, like a person with idiosyncratic behavioral patterns, unusual physical characteristics, or a tendency to over- or under-emote." The list of identifiers is hardly clear. What is idiosyncratic or unusual? And who gets to judge what is over- or under-emoting? The Slate journalist offers some specifics to clarify: "People were creeped out by those who repeatedly licked their lips; laughed at inappropriate moments; and habitually steered their conversations toward a single subject, particularly sex."[5] Again, we might agree that some of these are creepy behaviors, but the list doesn't really get us any closer to isolating what creeps people out consistently, which suggests that our creep is a moving target and the creepiness detector itself an idiosyncratic application.

With that said, there are some things we can assert confidently about creepiness. For instance, note, in the quotation above, the use of the pronoun "she" as the possessor of the "creepiness detector," which, even if used to signal an aversion to relying on "he" as the stand-in for all humanity, still powerfully registers that men are far more likely to be found to be creepy, and women the objects of their creeping. I see this kind of creepiness all the time. At one of the coffee shops I frequent, the boss, probably about 30, regularly comes in and starts talking to his "girls," says he's going to watch them while they work, asks them if they are best friends. Watching these interactions, I realize I'm seeing the creepiness of male privilege. He's the boss, so the young women are playing along, and he's a man, so he's probably not even aware that he's being creepy—or doesn't care. He could even be showing off a bit, knowing that I'm sitting a few feet away, a regular. He's staking his claim to these young people. But more than that, I wonder what he's really thinking. I catch a glimpse of it, something sexual, but I'm not entirely sure. Is he just fooling around? Or does he have more sinister intent, wanting to use his power over these young people to sexualize the workplace? The sexually inappropriate is one of our most significant creep triggers, one made all the creepier because the intent of the creeper isn't quite known. Indeed, it's the potential for the inappropriate crossing of boundaries that most readily elicits a ping on the creep detector.

5 Christina Cauterruci, "What Makes Someone Creepy, According to Science," *Slate*, November 16, 2016, http://www.slate.com/blogs/xx_factor/2016/04/05/what_people_find_creepy_according_to_one_new_survey.html.

"Why Do We Creep On Our Exes?" takes a more sympathetic approach, arguing that "we all do it" and that it can even be "healthy," allowing us an opportunity to reflect on a relationship that has ended and slowly get some distance.[6] Also, we're a naturally curious species, so who can blame us? Some creepiness is even proactively defensive. One article asks how far women will go to "creep someone online" as a way of checking out potential partners. Such women are often responding to guys who have asked them out or expressed interest, and women supposedly creep in order to determine how "creepy" the interested parties might be.[7] Of course, creeping gets creepy if it's prolonged, limits personal growth, and turns into stalking. I appreciate this article's attempt to acknowledge at least the pervasiveness and relative harmlessness of certain kinds of creepy behavior, but the slope into stalking is a slippery one, suggesting that creeping is a habit best worth keeping in check. To be sure, numerous articles suggest that "you might be a creep and not even know it."[8] Do you stare at people just a bit too much? Or, conversely, do you fail to make sufficient eye contact? And most importantly, do you initiate sexualized conversation or make dirty comments in inappropriate settings? Creepiness isn't confined to what you (or others) might do in public, consciously or not, but also emerges as the *possibility* that you might be "staring" at someone without them knowing about it, such as "creeping" on your exes through social media. You don't have to be called out to be a creep — which makes creepiness such a capacious

6 Marlena Ahearn, " Why Do We Creep on Our Exes? It's More Complicated Than You Think," *Bustle,* November 17, 2016, https://www.bustle.com/articles/195351-why-do-we-creep-on-our-exes-its-more-complicated-than-you-think.

7 Ebony-Renee Baker, "We Asked Women How Far They'll Go to Creep Someone Online," *Vice,* August 19, 2016, http://www.vice.com/en_ca/read/we-asked-women-how-far-theyll-go-to-creep-someone-online.

8 See, for instance, this article on a country music radio station's website, "ICYMI… You Might Be a Creep and Not Even Know It," originally aired October 2, 2016, http://www.country1067.com/audio/icymi-might-creep-not-even-know/, which wonders if you "might be a creep and not even know it."

category. Indeed, we are never just looking out for other creeps, attempting to protect ourselves, but also monitoring *ourselves* to determine if our behavior is creepy. Such disciplining of other *and self* distributes the possibility of creepiness throughout the social field, saturating not just our encounters with others but our own sense of self with the threat of creepiness.

That saturation is often intensified in particular *spaces,* where the creep potential is heightened. As just one among many examples I'll be exploring in this book, I could talk about how I visit the same bathroom over and over, a public bathroom near where I work. I've never had sex in it, never masturbated in it, don't get hard in it, don't find it arousing in any overtly and even mildly sexual way. But I love sauntering up to the urinal, always giving dudes around me their space, and taking a piss with other people. I acknowledge that, to some, perhaps even a little bit to myself, my consistent and self-consciously active visitation of this particular restroom might be slightly creepy. For while I don't intend ever to sexualize overtly the space of this bathroom, I do enjoy being around other guys taking a piss. The intimacy of it is exciting. We're all holding our cocks together. Granted, others don't know I'm thinking this, but if they did, they'd likely be creeped out, except for the few who would totally be turned on — and that might creep me out a little bit.

Public restrooms are one of those spaces were the possibility of being or becoming perceived as creepy is enhanced, perhaps because it's a public space in which one's genitals are potentially exposed; at the very least, you're holding them for a bit. The installation of privacy screens between urinals oddly attests to a recognition that guys might be creeping on each other — a recognition that seems directly collateral to the rise in tolerance, and hence cognizance, of the presence of gay men. And guys in general aren't wrong to wonder if the bathroom is a spot that is always potentially creeping toward the sexual. Historically, some gays used to frequent public restrooms for clandestine hookups, and too many homosexuals have been arrested for "public indecency," their lives often destroyed, when all they really wanted to do was get off together in a society that otherwise didn't provide them many opportunities to meet. Such a legacy is part of the popular consciousness, making a public bathroom a potentially fraught space for straight men.

And ultimately, it's the fraught nature of a space that might contribute to the identification of creepy behavior or people as creeps themselves. We all learn, mostly, how to navigate different social spaces, and when we confuse or mix up behavior accepted in one space with that accepted in another, we run the risk of being creepy. If I tried actively to check out a guy's package in the restroom, I'd be creepy. But so too is the coffee shop owner who is flirting with his female staff being creepy. In the former case, I'd be overtly sexualizing a space where the sexual is supposed to be (and indeed has often been literally) policed and elided; in the latter, the boss is sexualizing the workplace and, moreover, taking advantage of his power position over his employees.

As we'll see, the sexually inappropriate hovers closely around much identification or perception of creepiness, though it isn't absolutely necessary for a behavior of person to be identified as creepy. Still, I'm very aware that my gayness has, historically at least, put me in the company of those all too readily identified as creepy, as those who push boundaries, behave inappropriately, and are just downright unnatural.

Curiously, that unnaturalness, even the specter of the creepy, is for many not just threatening, but exciting — exciting perhaps in the possibility of threat. Yes, we get creeped out. But we are also fascinated by creeps, perhaps in part because we all sense the possibility inside ourselves for creepy behavior. Marketers know this phenomenon and some have used it, as in a strange but striking advertisement for Diesel shoes, in which an old man creeps down to lick a younger man's footwear.[9] A commentator at the Propaganda for Change blog, which takes a critical look at a variety of persuasive media, readily identifies the old man as "creepy." But so too, I'd argue, is the young man, using his left foot to push down the older man's neck. And maybe so are we for looking at this ad and potentially finding it somewhat... intriguing. "Yes, I want my tennis shoes to dominate others," the ad seems to call out to you. Or at the very least, the advertisers suggest that wearing these shoes might empower you, even in a vaguely sexualized way. Surely, sex has been used to sell for a long time. But this is *creepy* sex. Apparently, some marketers are willing to bank on it selling too.

So, creepiness seems to surround us—in marketing and throughout social media, in the subtle sense of threat lurking in encounters with strangers, encounters most of us probably have on a daily basis. More personally, creepiness for me seems not just a lurking potential but also a pressing matter of *identity*—in large part because I grew up thinking I was creepy, probably like many gay men of my generation growing up in the Deep South with little access to gay subculture. We were told again and again that the feelings we had for other boys were wrong, dangerous, damning, and even deadly. And indeed, for much of the twentieth century, homosexuality and creepiness went hand in hand, bedfellows in the popular imagination that saw queer sexuality as a threat to normalcy, even an attack on the American way of life. In the 1950s, public service announcements, such as "Boys Beware," featured clearly creep men offering rides to unsuspecting boys, charmed by the offer of gifts and friendship. What's perhaps even creepier about such videos is the way in which the

9 For a picture of the original Diesel ad, see Arthur Chan, "A Creepy Old Man Will Lick Your Shoes," *Propaganda for Change,* February 14, 2013, http://persuasion-and-influence.blogspot.com/2013/02/a-creepy-old-man-will-lick-your-shoes.html.

warnings also targeted the young men too, suggesting that they needed to be on guard not just against the creep's advances but because they too could be "turned" into creeps. They might be bent toward queerness. The creep is never just a danger from outside; creepiness always lurks within as well.[10] I grew up with such fears, worrying over my sexuality, wondering when others would discover my creepiness.

Because of the intense homophobia surrounding my childhood and adolescence, my life was damaged, a botched job, from nearly its start. I just didn't realize it at the time. The damage would appear in time, revealing itself at some point after it was already too late for me to go back and try to correct what had been done, what had been set in motion. What was done? The sustained rejection I experience has become partially internalized as a constant voice that imagines, as robustly and insistently as possible, the constant possibility of future rejection. I ceaselessly second guess every planned encounter with another human being. Will this person keep his word? Will that person actually show up? How will she try to hurt me? I imagine myself always rejected ahead of time, abandoned but with cause, the creep outcast.

Some of us ceaselessly narrate our victimization. I rehearse, as you will see, more than a bit of mine in these pages. But what if, at some point, we were to tell the story of how we left someone else bereft, damaged, fucked? I'm proud that the damage I've caused has — I hope — been less than that done to me. But I have also wanted to confess, both to understand what I've learned from a culture's predation on one of its young and the ways in which I, too, have become something of creep.

10 An example of a "1950's Anti-Homosexual PSA" can be found on "1950's Anti-Homosexual PSA — Boys Beware," *YouTube* video, 10'12", posted by Devin Lieberman, December 3, 2010, https://www.youtube.com/watch?v=17u01_sWjRE. Plenty more are readily available online.

In part, this book documents that creepiness — how I came to it, how it shapes my sense of the world and myself as a sexual being, but also how it might be, at its best, a mode of critique. I have few pretensions about this, though. Not all creepiness can — or should — be salvaged by the possibility of it offering insight and fodder for intellectual consideration. Some creepiness, as noted, is just creepiness. But I have attempted in these pages to write from the inside, to explore my embodied perceptions, to confront if not necessarily resolve emotional conflicts. In writing his simultaneously scholarly and at times excruciatingly painful exploration of *Humiliation,* Wayne Koestenbaum describes the fundamental humiliation (and creepiness) of writing itself: "Writing is a process of turning myself inside out: a regurgitation. I extrude my vulnerable inner lining. I purge. And then I examine the contents — my expulsed interior — and begin the bloody interrogation. I ask whether is it filthy or clean, valuable or deplorable."[11] Following suit in my own fashion, I've wanted to see my inner creep. I want you to see him too — as creepy as that in itself might be — because you might understand yourself better in the process. We all might understand ourselves better if we see our own creepiness.

In a way, then, this is a memoir masquerading as theory, or what I have come to call critical memoir. It combines details from various scenes in my life with meditations on a variety of media that might help illuminate our fascination with creepiness. Like all memoirists, I've allowed myself to indulge a bit of suggestive self-fabulation and mythologizing. I don't pretend to reach the heights of biomythography, Audre Lorde's term for her work in *Zami,* which so lovingly and critically intertwines the personal and the political.[12] But I do indulge my own moments of critique, or at least allow them to creep up on you, the reader (if you'll pardon the first of many such puns). At its worst, my nar-

11 Wayne Koestenbaum, *Humiliation* (New York: Picador, 2011), 17

12 Audre Lorde, *Zami: A New Spelling of My Name* (Trumansburg: Crossing Press, 1982).

rations and explorations here might be a narcissistic loop that spins itself into periodic knots that I struggle to untie. If I can't untie some of them, tough, I think they'd unravel not just me but a culture that ties some of us up in the tangles of self-hatred. In these pages, I at least try.

A Life

"Your childhood
is the foundation
of the system."
—d. a. levy

I was a creepy kid. Or at least that's what I'm told. Physically, the odds were already stacked a bit against me. I was (and still am) cross-eyed, and apparently, my head was alarmingly large—so large that the ophthalmologist my parents took me to about my crossed eyes suggested that I be taken immediately to a physician to be examined for a brain tumor. I did not (and don't believe I have) a brain tumor. But, in my child version, something was still... amiss.

Other parents wouldn't let their children play with me. I'm not entirely sure why. The large head and odd eyes may have been concerning. But also, my mother was reading works by Dr. Spock and other child psychologists, works that, in the late '60s and early '70s, advised against corporally punishing children and suggested other modes of less intrusive and more nurturing forms of correction and discipline. Other children staying away might have been their parents' way of showing disapproval for how my mother was raising me, as well as my first sister, born four years after me.

But beyond the physical oddities and potential parental skepticism, I suspect I was (as I am still) just strange. I remember lots of solitary games. When mother would take me to the store on a weekly shopping trip, I'd apparently beg and beg, howling in sore need, for spools of thread. Mother had a sewing machine and I recall sitting at it for hours, stitching lines of thread into material over and over. Those spools of thread were also often used as power lines for electrical poles made of Tinker Toys that would span Fischer Price and wooden block cities. To this day, I don't know why I'm not an architect, as some of my fondest memories of childhood are of these immense cities that I would build—built landscapes with Little Golden Books as roofs and Hot Wheels rubber tracks as elevated freeways—that would cover the living room floor. Legos and then an Erector Set steadily helped sophisticate my feats of miniature civil engineering. I am, instead, a teacher.

Perhaps like many others, I also remember a lot of late childhood tie-up games. I must've been influenced by the Adam West *Batman* because the neighbor kid and I would use bed sheets as capes and slide our tighty-whities over our pants and tie each other up, cackling with delight as we taunted each other to escape our bonds before the bomb went off and destroyed everything. The neighborhood kids and I spent a lot of time tying up the preacher's kid—he seemed to like it; I know I did. And my sister and I, me upon the cusp of puberty, would don those tighty-whities and play superheroes. I'd be captured and tortured, the hero struggling in jump rope bonds while instructing my sister to belt me harder to make me reveal the secrets required to reign destruction down on us all. *BAM! KerPOW!*

From what I've heard, though, the ropes and thread had more nefarious uses as well. I'm told I made trip wires, catching my parents unawares. My parents would hear gleeful laughs coming from around the corner. And then, in a more intensely apocryphal story, as my sister lay in her crib, I supposedly tied a noose around her neck, the other end of the thread attached to a doorknob that I would open and close, listening to her choke. I have no memories of these events. I remember the cities, building and, of course, launching block bombs when my mother told me I had to clean up the mess. But the trip wires and choking are stories told to *me*, even *about me*. Apparently, I was a creepy kid.

And, of course, I remember the tie-up games. The first time I ever achieved orgasm I had tied myself up. I must've been 11 or 12, in middle school, alone in my room in the afternoon, still in my khaki schoolboy uniform, watching cartoons (early anime, I think, *Battle of the Planets*), my cheap leather belts becoming my bonds as I lay face down, struggling, wriggling, rubbing, and oh shit what was that? I recall a pleasant and unsettling shiver, some emanating heat, a throb. I don't remember any fluid. But I do remember thinking that maybe I shouldn't do this again. At least until tomorrow. And for a decade I masturbated primarily through frottage, both with and without self-bondage.

Yes, I'm something of a sadomasochist, though now, approaching 50 and the steady leaching of testosterone from my body, I'm less propelled to play or fantasize such games. Still, in my day, I've been a pretty twisted fucker, if largely in my own mind. The Adam West *Batman* certainly made an impression on my childhood polymorphous perversity. The satiny capes and shiny trunks have become fetish objects for me. And the regularity with which the duo—a seemingly savvy older man and his youthful and admiring sidekick—found themselves in precarious bondage has influenced many a sexual narrative I've scripted and run in the porno theater of my mind, and occasionally acted out. As a kid, board games became opportunities for perverse little bets. Risk was a perpetual favorite, and it seemed only appropriate that the loser would somehow be subject to the whims of the world-conquering victor. Light bondage and even spankings augmented many afternoon gaming sessions. Such mildly erotic play, never resulting in actual full-on sexual contact, persisted into early adulthood. I would stay up late into the night, playing games with friends, subjecting each other to various humiliations in the name of motivating better game play. I can make no comment about my friends' enjoyment, but I've often been surprised by what a straight guy will consent to do, as long as you don't make him feel too self-conscious about it.

And like many kids, I had my own imaginary friends, Mont and Dant. I don't remember them well, but their names have stuck with me for over four decades. I don't recall what we would do, though I think they liked thread too. I was well into my 20s when someone pointed out, perhaps my ex-wife who is a therapist, that Mont and Dant are clearly stand-ins for Mom and Dad. Well duh. But why did I need parental stand-ins? My mother was raising us as a stay-at-home mom; Dad worked for the local power company, but he was generally home in the evenings. I remember them being around, surely. What do I remember?

My parents bought me all sorts of sport gear, and I have vague recollections of suiting up in pads, jersey, and helmet, carrying a football outside while kids ran away in horror. I likely exaggerate here. I mean, the uniform I remember, and a scattering of bodies. But were they *fleeing*? I'm not sure. That part of the narrative gets mixed up between what I remember and what I've been told.

Indeed, I think my mother sometimes enjoys embellishing my past. She has told me that I once bit a young girl. I think I was in kindergarten. She had apparently spit on me. When mother told me this story a couple of years ago, a story of which I have absolutely no memory, my body convulsed a laugh of triumph out of me. The little bitch, she deserved to be bit. What I remember, though, is a faint memory of a smiling girl with pigtails, flower spotted cotton dress. Was she the one hurling her spit at me?

My mother is also the one who told me about how men and women have vaginally penetrative sex, after I'd seen something on television that sparked my curiosity—some pristine sexual health cartoon typical of the '70s. I was 12, I think. I remember some slight discomfort at the thought, more a distaste, a souring in the mouth. The way *she* told it, however, I was puking into the garbage can. I overheard her tell such a tale to one of the parents who'd come to pick up her child from the nursery my mother operated on the first floor of our home (more on this nursery later). Why would she say such a thing? I didn't puke. If anything, my outward demeanor was — I'm sure — somewhat nonchalant as I trudged back up the stairs to tie myself up and rub out an orgasm. But I was perplexed by her lie. Was she trying to normalize me? Was I *supposed* to feel that sex was somehow disgusting? I thought it — sex — certainly *strange*. But I wouldn't go so far as to say that what she described grossed me out. Could she have read my apparent sanguinity as a kind of *creepiness*? Perhaps I came across as too worldly, too knowing, and needed, at least for outward appearances, some kind of normalizing gesture. But is disgust at sex *normal*? Weirdly, in my mind such a story gets caught up with another incident, sitting across from some newly met gay male friends; we're in our 30s and talking, inevitably, about sexual practices, and I mention that I'd been married and had actually enjoyed vaginally penetrative sex with my wife, and some of the guys' lips twisted in shock and horror. Ewww. *How could you stand that*? *Disgusting*! I guess that, even among some gays, I'm capable of creeping people out.

To this day, my mother will pick on me, or on the strange kid I once was. (I think she's a bit more cautious around the strange adult I've become.) I will still hear stories of how I was a mean kid. I used to be sweet. But the uniform of normal boyhood never quite fit. As she put it once, in a moment of kindness, I was trying to figure myself out. And she's probably right.

Oh, there were many signs that I was… *unique*, in need of figuring out. People were reading those signs all around me. In a mall in Biloxi, I bought a book and plopped down a five-dollar bill, apparently with some flourish and aplomb. This was the first time I was buying a book on my own as a kid. My mother, watching in horror from the sidelines, later informed me that I'd totally embarrassed the young female clerk. I shouldn't be so "dramatic." Such early lessons in the embarrassing spectacle of my gender nonconformity were re-enforced throughout my youth, not just in the torture chambers of my high school gym, my lack of coordination constantly calling me out as less than manly, but also in well-meaning older folk, such as a father whose kids I babysat who noticed I was reading a book by Truman Capote and wondered if I was "trying to tell us something."

Besides my architectural fantasies, various light bondage, and some unfortunate concoctions mixed together from a chemistry set, my most common form of childhood entertainment revolved around playing school. I can't remember the first time that I played school, but I think I did so until I was at least 14, drafting the kids in the neighborhood and my mother's nursery into my schoolrooms. I was always the teacher. I would concoct multi-day curricula, detailed lesson plans, quizzes and examinations for which I used carbon paper to reproduce. The delicious sticky stink of purple ink is still something of a turn on. You used to be able to buy remaindered textbooks at what we called "drug stores," the forebears of Walgreen's and CVS. I quivered with anticipation on trips to such stores, hunting for the cache of $1 books. Subject and grade level were irrelevant. I collected scores of these textbooks and would use them to compose curricula in math, reading, geography. Then back at the house, my sister and her friends would be subject to my tutelage. I took the play teaching quite seriously, but I also loved the paraphernalia of instruction. Out of old boxes and Tinker Toys, I made large flip charts to reveal the mysteries of sentence diagramming. I used my old Erector Set to try to make a chalk holder, one of those delightful contraptions that a teacher could fill with a stick of chalk while keeping her hands clean from the dusty substance. I fucking loved chalkboards. We had a large one in the nursery, and I spent many days just drawing on it. The swipe of an eraser across the black surface seemed miraculous, especially if it was soundless. Everything clear. Nothing more to see here.

Once, an early memory, I was playing school in a set of large refrigerator boxes, my makeshift schoolrooms. I'd dragooned a neighbor boy, a kid with a delightful British accent, into playing my pupil. I was probably 9 or so, he 7, and we'd already had our superhero fantasy play, me stuffing my football jersey into my briefs pulled over my pajama bottoms to protect the household from the Joker. The kid seemed eager for anything. But for some reason, my mother came to pull him out of the box, yelling at me that she had already warned me not to play school with this boy. I still feel her stinging slap, less on my upper arm and more on my mind. I wasn't sure what was wrong. We were just playing. I don't recall anything strange. Unless playing school itself constituted something untoward.

Surely in time the untoward would emerge. One of the rituals of schooling I enjoyed most was meting out punishment. I was always sending one of my students to the corner. And eventually a ruler was randomly and regularly applied to the buttocks of a variety of neighborhood kids. I wouldn't hit my sister, though. If she misbehaved, I made her read passages from the Bible in detention. But her male friend would get a stern spanking. Again, no one seemed to mind, although we all knew to keep such play to ourselves, behind the closed doors of our rooms.

I'm surprised that so much of my childhood play focused on school, though maybe not surprised that I always insisted on playing the teacher. I would let other kids spank me, but not as nearly as often as I wielded the rod of correction. And to be fair, this was hardly just all pre-pube kink play. Real scholastic activity occurred. I somehow loved teaching, with the accompanying design of lessons, pedagogical activities, and assessments, which suggests I somehow loved learning. But my experiences with *actual* school weren't as playful. Indeed, *real* school was something of a traumatic space for me.

I barely remember kindergarten, and nothing particularly tragic. Loud and noisy rooms, naptime, making various craft objects. But first grade was a shitshow. We'd moved to a new house in Metairie, a large suburban community outside New Orleans, and the school, a public school, Alice Burney, was just a block from my parents' home, which I could see from the playground. I spent many recess periods crying at the chain-linked fence, wailing to go home. It seems that one teacher would be set to supervise hundreds of kids as they roamed the playground in their feral ways, so I barely recall catching that teacher's notice, though I remember my mother coming up to the fence and trying to figure out why I was so distressed.

Part of it was her fault, though not maliciously so. My mother had apparently enrolled me a bit late and so I couldn't be placed into one room with one teacher who could guide her class throughout the day. Instead, I had to roam from class to class, learning reading in one room, math in another, etc., etc. In retrospect, none of this makes sense to me, and I can't imagine that anyone thought this was a good accommodation. It meant, in effect, that I never got to know any set of kids particularly well, shuttled as I was from space to space. Beyond my large-headedness, I was spatially marked as the odd one out, the freak, an outsider.

So, I started acting out. In one room, I don't remember the subject but it was clearly some art-oriented activity, I started eating paper. We were making bones to arrange into skeletons for a Halloween project, and, instead of making my ghoul, I took to ingesting my art supplies. I'm sure I freaked the teacher out. This behavior did not help to alleviate the other kids' — or the teachers' — sense that I was a budding creep.

But the largest part of my distress I lay at the feet of Ms. W. (I actually remember her name to this day, even if I won't use it here.) She taught reading, and I clearly vexed her. I'm not entirely sure why. One event — I must have been all of six years old — is emblazoned on my mind. On the first day of class, all of our school supplies, which our parents had to buy and send us to school with on the first day, were taken from us and put into communal piles, to be used socialistically throughout the school year. So, one day, when we were assigned a coloring activity, a fellow student was given the coffee can of crayons and instructed to provide us each with a set of colors. This little girl didn't care for me, for what reason I do not know. I suspect my large head and tendency to eat paper didn't help, so, when she came to my desk she only gave me black and orange crayons. I started to protest, she pulled away, and I stood up to assert my right to additional colors beyond black and orange. Ms. W. was furious and sent me to the corner. Again, I tried to protest, but she was having none of it. I was clearly in the wrong.

I don't remember all the ways in which I communicated my displeasure and creeping sense of injustice at the world. I was only a child after all; my resources for revenge were limited, and I'd already tried biting, but one sticks out. During lunch, as Ms. W. sat at the head of a freakishly long table while all of her charges wolfed down their food, I calmly left my place, walked up to her, and, as she sat there wondering what the hell I wanted, quietly pissed my pants. She just shook her head in disgust. I had won. Even today, as I write this, I chuckle with the memory of victory.

This was my one and only year at Alice Burney. My parents then moved us from the suburbs to the country, a river town called St. Rose about an hour outside the city, where they bought a condominium and I was enrolled in a Catholic school, St. Charles Bormeo, and my parents sent me to a child psychologist, who promptly told them that the problem was that I was too intelligent, under-stimulated, and that they would have to adapt to my needs. I don't think they were impressed by this. But neither had a college education, and while both were quite intelligent, they didn't have many options, strategies, and resources for dealing with a strange child. Sending me to Catholic schools — smaller classes, better teachers — was a way to help provide better education than they had had. It was also mildly racist. Throughout my entire Catholic education — attending from second grade through high school — I knew perhaps three black kids. Three. In an area with a very large African-American population. My parents just didn't want us hanging around the blacks. So, addressing my creepiness by sending me to Catholic schools could also scratch a racist itch.

Am I being harsh? Perhaps. But my memories of schooling, even in — and perhaps especially in — the Catholic schools would come to make the one-year at Alice Burney actually seem educational. For sure, I learned a lot from the Catholics, who apparently did have a more rigorous curriculum of book learning. But their schools were also the site of intense abuse and bullying for me — and not just at the hands of other students. So, in retrospect, the acting out I experimented with at Alice Burney — an acting out that seems now like justifiable protest — was slowly beaten out of me, if not always physically then most definitely psychically.

Part of my initial difficulty in these schools might have arisen out of the fact that I wasn't Catholic. As a Cajun growing up in southwest Louisiana, my mother was raised Catholic, but upon getting married to my religiously unaffiliated father by the justice of the peace, her priest began refusing her the sacraments. (Because that's how their god rolls.) So, while we were surrounded by Catholics and were growing up in a very Catholic-influenced culture — Mardi Gras being an uber-Catholic kind of event, a hedonic blowout before forty days of self-depriving Lent in anticipation of the celebration of the execution and resurrection of Christ — we as a family had opted out of that particular religion. (In time, we would become Southern Baptists, initiating its own particular trajectory of terror. More on this later.) So, all of my friends and pretty much all of my classmates were learning and participating in rituals that explicitly excluded me. Actually, I learned the rituals; I just couldn't take part in their official practice. We learned about the terrors of the confessional and the mysteries of the Eucharist, and kids would line up at the large wooden boxes to give confessing a go and then practice taking unconsecrated Eucharist, either delicately extending the tongue or piously holding up clean hands. I'd sit and watch, having been quizzed on my knowledge of the rituals but denied their experience. To be fair, I was allowed to go talk to the priests in a kind of confession, but it was clear to me — and to all others — that I was separate, different, perhaps even damned. Good job, educators!

My second through sixth grades passed in this state of semi-spiritual exile. Many times, at recess, I would circumnavigate a large oak tree, circling it again and again for the entire hour, stepping carefully over its complex and exposed root system, imagining them as highways around a large city, the Tinker Toys and wooden blocks of my earlier childhood projected onto this living entity. No teacher came up to me to inquire, and most students just left me alone. I wasn't engaging others much, and I mostly sat quietly in class, outcast but not troubling anyone, while other kids would coyly bop up to the priest prowling the play yard, asking "Father, may I have some candy?" which he'd then dole out of his trouser pockets. Perhaps I was already learning the value of trying to keep out of sight, lest my protests of black and orange crayons send me once again to the corner. Perhaps I was already just putting myself in the corner automatically, before enduring the humiliation of being told to go there. After all, some of the nuns had little paddles and while I didn't mind spanking other kids I most certainly didn't want to be on the receiving end of a sex-deprived menopausal woman's wrath. (I'm obviously glossing with my middle-aged sense of things, but still…)

For middle school (seventh and eighth grades) we moved and I had to switch schools again, and then again go to a separate parochial high school. Entering middle school coincided with the onset of puberty, and the predatory nature of childhood assumed a whole new set of chemically induced imperatives. All of a sudden, my non-Catholic, vaguely Aspergery, non-engaging, solitude-seeking, keeping-under-the-radar nerdiness had a name. *Faggot.* It actually had several names, including gay, homo, and queer, but fag and faggot quickly became my new names. The sexualizing of childhood predation isn't surprising. We were all feeling the flux and fumbling throbs of flesh, although I don't know how many of my fellow classmates were tying themselves up as a prelude to rubbing one off. But I suspect a few were. I distinctly remember one kid, a gangly dark-skinned boy with a shock of kinky hair who grabbed the teacher's ruler once and started whaling on his own ass before the befuddled matron could grab it away from him. I had neither the nerve nor the wherewithal to invite him over to play after school, though I wish I had.

Instead I was too busy dodging the verbal attacks of my classmates, coming from both boys and girls, and trying to make myself small and unnoticeable. Fortunately, though, I was a tall kid, and I think my height served as a kind of frontline deterrent for physical assault. I was rarely physically attacked, but that may be because my fellow students just weren't paying enough attention. I was clearly inept at PE, and I was always chosen last when captains were brutally instructed to divvy us up into teams, so anyone could've seen that I wasn't capable of defending a corporeal assault. I couldn't do pushups. I couldn't do pull-ups. I was always last in a race.

But I was also, at the time, a tattle-tale. Once I was shoved roughly and tripped down part of a flight of stairs. I told my parents who exhorted me to fight back, to defend myself. I responded by saying that Christ instructs us to turn the other cheek. Their mouths hung open.

Certainly, I had *some* friends, and I suppose in some ways my childhood was marked by scrapes not *too* uncharacteristic of others'. I didn't play with fire, but I did steal the neighbors' mail once. He was so fucking pissed. I also abused a cat once, and feel bad about it to this day. Nothing terrible really. I just picked it up and flung it around. It wasn't hurt though probably scared to death, maybe traumatized by the sight of children from then on. I did befriend some fellow sufferers, like a Russian kid whose parents had defected from the USSR, another outsider, someone everyone else picked on too. We huddled together, pretending we had things in common. I suppose we did. But years later — and I mean like three decades — I found him online, living just up the road about an hour away, suggested we have dinner, and it was a total disaster. He'd become a Republican, fairly conservative, and his wife scowled at me throughout the dinner; I kept wondering if she was wondering what this faggot wanted with her husband, and *oh my god why didn't you tell me you had a gay friend when you were younger.* He barely remembered me, though. Well, he *did*, but he'd moved on to other friends after going to a different high school, his adolescence filled with the usual and the normal, leaving a safe and secure taste in his mouth as he lifted another bit of expensive steak to his pristine teeth. I asked after his younger sister, and the wife erupted: *Am I going to contact her out of the blue too? What, really, do you want?* She didn't ask that last part, but she was clearly thinking it. I could feel it. I felt the force of the question too. What *do* I want? Why did I reach out? A gap opens up, a chasm of unknowable intention. It's dark in there, even to me. Why should it not be dark to others, and a little bit scary because of that lack of light, that unfathomable need that calls out to others, come in, come in?

My father… you might be wondering where he's been. If I have delayed in introducing my parents more fully that might have to do with my retrospective sense of them as largely absent from my childhood. Of course, that's just patently bullshit. Nothing could be further from the truth. They were around, all the time. But I have had to contend with the fact that, walking in circles around and around a tree alone in a playground full of kids, I experienced my childhood largely by myself. And then increasingly, picked on and bullied, teased and tormented, made even further outcast, I don't wonder that I spent some afternoons tying myself up.

My father did show up one day at my school when I was in seventh grade to talk to the principal about the bullying I was experiencing. I was called into her office and there he sat. I don't know if the surprise I felt was felt at the moment I saw him, or if I remember surprise through the years of all the times he didn't show up, or both. I do remember going through the door and pulling up short when I saw him turn around to face me, the strange, large headed outcast child he'd come to somehow protect. I wonder what he was thinking. He was in his work clothes, taking a half hour out of his day to stand up for the son who had elected to turn the other cheek. Did he resent being there? Or is that resentment all mine, a backwards feeling into this encounter that stands out for me because it is so anomalous, so not how I would experience my father throughout my life?

I learned from my mother years later, in my late 30s, after he had died, that, when I was born, my father wondered if I was actually his. I must have been a monstrous looking baby. But that little revelation, whatever he really thought, just learning of his suspicion, allowed me to see my childhood in a glaringly new light. His distance, his lack of engagement, his coldness — they all made sense. I don't ever recall playing with my father. I remember him drying my and my sister's hair after a bath. We must have been 8 and 4. He took the towel, roughly drying my hair and then, taking both ends, rubbed it furiously across the back of my neck, giving me a brush burn. I yelped up out of his reach. To this day, my body stores tension in my neck.

Years later, just days before I got married to a lovely young woman — a soul similar in her feelings of being an outcast, an outsider in her own right — he asked if I was homosexual.

To be sure, he showed up for the typical things: graduations, and the wedding. Mother told me, perhaps right around the same time that he asked if I was queer, that he was sad he didn't have a part to play in the wedding. But by that point, I didn't know what role to give him. Years later, after I was already divorced and starting to date the man I would eventually marry, he called me up on the phone — the only time he ever did — to ask if I believed in god. He was dying of Parkinson's disease, slowly, devastatingly, losing one bodily function, including his mind, after another, all the while taking my mother down into despair with him. By that point, I didn't believe in god—not in any conventional way. But I was taken up in the strangeness of the call, its truly exceptional character, a one-of-a-kind and probably never-to-be-repeated (it wasn't) event. I stammered a reply: if there is a god, I can't imagine he wouldn't be full of forgiveness, even if only for having made us and allowing us to suffer so much. Indeed, if he had any moral sense and wasn't cosmically psychotic, god should be asking *our* forgiveness. My father seemed satisfied with this response. The tremor in his voice, the dual shaking of body and heart, a soul sensing its own imminent demise, stilled a bit before hanging up.

I must have been a profound disappointment. Why else would he have turned away from me for so long, calling only when his own pain drove him to ask for succor from someone he had largely ignored? Am I misreading that phone call? To this day, nearly twenty years later, I don't know. Maybe that call was the respect and love he'd always felt but couldn't show because of his own damage, his own emotional stuntedness. I don't know.

But that's telling, because I know next to nothing about him. He married late, in his early 30s, and yes, that was late for that time period. (My mother was 24 when she had me.) I know he came from a large family, eight brothers and sisters, and tried to dodge the draft during the Korean War, not out of any sense of peacenik protest, but because, shit, who wants to go to war? He worked most of his life for the power company. He drove a truck and, if you didn't pay your electric bill, he was the one charged with turning off your power. He hated his job. He was often yelled out, cussed out, sometimes attacked by dogs at their owners' command. He tried to cheat his work, coming home in the early afternoons for long naps while still on the clock. He was eventually caught and told he'd be fired if he were caught doing this again. He took his resentments out in other ways, such as going to discount clothing stores on the weekends, buying name-brand shirts, and then taking them to higher-end stories and returning them as unwanted gifts for cash. (Something you can't do anymore without gift receipts.) I actually admire the ingenuity he had, even as I'm left wondering what drove him to feel he deserved to cheat others.

We barely knew his brothers and sisters. There was a crazy one, subjected to electric shock treatments in the state mental hospital, having gone around the bend after much of her body suffered third-degree burns in a mysterious house fire. A largely toothless one. A fairly malignant one. A younger brother who disappeared. Another aunt I only recall meeting once because she got the fuck out of southern Mississippi, married, had children, made a life elsewhere. Right after 9/11, she started mailing my father and one of his other brothers threatening letters, demanding payment for therapy services to deal with the trauma of having been sexually abused by them. Everything was denied, a lawyer consulted, the letters ignored, the correspondence slowly stopping. It was all, in a word, creepy, or at least suggested dark secrets from the past slowly creeping into the present. To this day, we don't know what the truth is.

I had little time as a child, though, to meditate on my parents' varied and potentially sordid pasts. High school was generally a horror for me. There's little other way to say it. I went to an all-boys Catholic school, where I believe I got a solid education, was introduced to a slew of good books and literature, and found a couple of teachers who encouraged my writing habit. But I faced nearly daily traumas of harassment, bullying, and abuse. I was immediately marked as the class fag, and I was verbally taunted all four years. Even some teachers, apparently, understood me as queer, sharing that information with students. I, of course, had made no such declaration. I think I barely said a word out loud. You have to keep in mind that this was in the early '80s, in the

Deep South; people just weren't very openly gay. Some of us suspected that a few of the brothers who helped run the school, and actually lived in separate housing on campus, might be queer, and I even heard from some students that one of the brothers in particular would diddle students on various academic tournament trips out of town. But this was all well before the priest abuse scandals, and also before the relatively widespread depiction of gays and lesbians on television and in movies. Being in Louisiana, and in a Catholic school, homosexuality just wasn't discussed. Even talking about it seemed dirty—unless you were identifying someone as a fag or faggot to ostracize him socially.

And that was me.

PE was a particular torture. I never showered on high school premises. To be fair, not many boys did. But I'm not going to lie here: for all of my deep shame at the time, and my sense of horror that I might in fact be a faggot, I was still a kid going through puberty. As I was surrounded by other boys going through puberty, I'd inevitably try to sneak a look at some of the boys changing in and out of their PE uniforms. We all wore white briefs (in fact, the coaches insisted on it, or a jockstrap), and to this day a lean muscled man in tighty-whities seems wonderfully erotic to me. (The Marky Mark Calvin Klein underwear ads posed a particular challenge to resist public gawking in the early '90s, outing myself on city streets as a real creep.)

But wait: more briefs, I remember, intimately interwoven into the narrative of my adolescent sexuality. At 16, 17, I snuck into the movies to see *Risky Business,* my first rated R film and I knew immediately that I wanted Tom Cruise. Not from the scene of him dancing around in his tighty-whities but the later one in which he's calling the prostitute while lying in those same briefs in his bed, pulling his goalie mask down over his head while he touches himself. Fuck that's hot, even now. I instantly had a crush on Cruise, and *Top Gun,* coming out just a few years later, seemed like pure porn to me. I hunted out other movies he starred in, or even just appeared in, including the pretty wretched *Cocktail*. When he was cast in *The Color of Money* with Paul Newman, *Life* magazine put their pictures on the front cover, lying head to head, and I bought a copy, poring over it secretly, relishing the article for glimpses into the actor's life. I still have that copy of *Life*. At school, studying alone in a classroom for a psychology test, I'd go to the chalkboard, writing out notes, then erasing them and writing "I love…" and then holding back from writing a name, but quickly scribbling "TC" before wiping the board clean. And while my interest in Cruise has since faded, and I haven't kept up with his filmography (that whole Scientology thing is just weird), I remember seeing him in the opening scenes of *Vanilla Sky*, standing bare chested in front of a mirror, searching for a gray hair before yanking it out. I yelped along with him, recognizing, in the late '90s, that I too was getting older. He's a few years older than I am, but close enough that tracking his aging has been instructive for my own. How *does* one get older, gracefully? And is that really the goal — grace?

Besides Tom Cruise, I had my first real crush on another human being in high school during sophomore year: Domingo. (We are Facebook friends to this day.) He was so fucking hot, though I'm not sure I could've brought myself to that exact articulation at the time. I was too busy trying to deflect attention from my sexuality, denying that I was, indeed, the faggot everyone seemed to think I was. So, my sensations seemed vaguer, less definable, but still surging. He wore a hot pink undershirt, with a button down over, barely tucked into his sand-colored khakis, and frequently sported a pea coat in winter. He was Latino, but very fair skinned, with a shock of black hair swooping over his forehead. He swaggered and was snide, quick-witted, and his friends were amongst the smartest kids in school. It was assumed that I was very smart too (bookish, bespectacled, literally egg-headed, quiet), but I didn't make friends with this smart set — who were all a little bit slick, sharp-tongued, well-dressed, and generally good-looking. Ah, the categories of adolescent education. I look back and think, if only I'd found a way to attract the attention of these boys, I might have found a somewhat safer harbor to weather the weirdness of high school. But it wasn't happening. I made some fumbling attempts to get to know Domingo, invited him over to listen to music. (I had not thought of a sexual encounter; I just wanted to be near him, perhaps wanted to *be* him.) He came over but thought I was just showing off my musical knowledge. (I'd hide in my room most afternoons and evenings, licking my wounds by listening to music.) Our friendship went nowhere, and I pined silently, eventually consoling myself by imagining tying him up and whipping his ass as I rubbed out an orgasm late at night. Who was I kidding? Of course I was a little faggot. But I was also deeply ashamed of being so and desperate still to hide, deflect, throw off the scent of others, however unsuccessfully. I eventually ran into Domingo again in college, where he and his friends had turned to evangelical Christianity; he remains a right-thinking Christian to this day, though he heard gracefully my admission to him, thirty years after the fact, that he was my first crush.

Teachers, except for a very few, were useless. Don't get me wrong: I think I got a decent humanistic education, perhaps with too much religion, but I still read good books, including some surprises like Ken Kesey's *One Flew Over the Cuckoo's Nest* and Herman Hesse's *Demian*, as well as the usual classics, such as *Lord of the Flies*. But most teachers seemed to turn a blind eye to the tortures I faced. I wasn't protected, and my parents, I think, just thought I needed to learn to man up and fight back. I did once. A kid took a small razor to me, wanting to carve "fag" into my arm, but I slapped his hand away and may have snarled. I remember the look of shock on his face. Perhaps that was enough to deter my fellow students from more probing physical assaults, and I was still tall, so perhaps unknown in terms of strength.

But no adult intervention was forthcoming. In fact, in a strange way, the school vectored such assaults — not only through its religious condemnation of anything sexually perverse (the only sex education we got was being shown pictures of aborted fetuses), but also by publishing our phone numbers in a widely distributed booklet. Perhaps they thought this would build community. It did, but mostly amongst those little budding sadists and future wife and child abusers who would get together and prank phone call my house. Prank phone call seems such a mild way of putting it. One kid called my house and told my mother that I was going to be beaten so badly that she wouldn't be able to buy groceries for a while because my hospital bills were going to be so high. I walked to and from school in fear. I think my parents alerted the school officials, but hey, what could they do? Boys will be boys. And people thought *I* was creepy.

In retrospect, I think I was abused. *Sexually* abused. While next to no one laid a hand on me, my sense of self was warped by a combination of social ostracism, religious intolerance, adult indifference, and ceaseless bullying. If I were a middle-class kid today, my parents would be trying to sue the school — and would likely be successful in securing a settlement. I've thought of doing such now. And for several years, in my late 20s, coming into consciousness of how what I'd faced had not been just boys being boys, I would write letters and then emails to my old high school's administrators. In part, my missives were in response to the periodic pleas for donations sent out by the school. Replying to one, I wrote the principal (a new guy, a lay person, not anyone I knew), saying that I'd consider donating money if the school set up a Gay — Straight Student Alliance. The possibility, though, was unthinkable for them, given Catholic doctrine. Is it any wonder that, for many years, I thought that anyone identifying themselves with Catholicism or Christianity were suspects? After all, they were aligned with a system of thought that, no matter their particular views on homosexuality, had contributed to the immiseration of countless millions for nearly two millennia. Fuck those fuckers, I'd think.

Anyway, I graduated, finally, disappointing my parents by deciding to study English in college. I wanted, oddly, to be a teacher. To be fair to my high school experience, I had a couple of teachers, one in particular, Ms. Morgavi, who encouraged my interest in reading and writing. I'd bring her my poetic attempts, and she said I should keep going. I clung to these bits of attention and stayed in touch with her for years afterwards, decades, well into my career and her eventual retirement from teaching.

Given my isolation, combined with a toxic brew of varied abuse and neglect, it's no exaggeration to say that reading probably saved my life. I'd actually done poorly in what was called language arts when in grade school, getting Bs and Cs, even meriting a deficiency one time — there was a warning that I was likely not to pass Reading. To earn extra credit, my fifth-grade teacher suggested I memorize and recite poems in front of the class. I did, performing several. They were amongst the only times I probably spoke aloud in school. But they probably also instilled in me, or helped develop, an interest in language. Then, one term, the same teacher read to us daily from C.S. Lewis's *The Lion, the Witch, and the Wardrobe*. I was hooked. By the end of the book, she was quizzing us, asking us if the story of Aslan's self-sacrifice for his friends reminded us of any other story. Clueless, we listened raptly while she explained that Lewis had essentially re-written the story of Christ's crucifixion as a fantasy. I was mesmerized. I couldn't have articulated the precise nature of my fascination, but I suspect the little boy I was, proto-queer, intuited that the doubleness of the story — saying one thing but meaning another, telling a tale with hidden depths — was a strategy with which I would become intimately familiar.

The fantasy of the story, as well as the power of reading to transport, were immediately useful, and I started reading as an escape. I haunted bookstores. The first book I read on my own was the sequel to *The Lion, the Witch, and the Wardrobe*, called *Prince Caspian*, and I still have that battered little book. I think it was the first book I actually bought too. I took it with me on our poor man's summer family vacation to Biloxi, where, when not burning my skin to a blistered crisp while building sand castles and swimming in polluted Gulf waters, I'd sit in our favorite beach-front McDonald's and read Prince Caspian. My father turned to me at one point: "You're not supposed to read on vacation. Vacation is for fun." I looked back down into my book and kept going, reading on the hour drive all the way back home.

After completing *The Chronicles of Narnia*, I scouted out the books next to it — other fantasies, then science fiction, delighting in long series, reading all of L. Frank Baum's Oz books, then Terry Brooks's *Sword of Shanara*, etc., etc. The books assigned in class I barely touched. Mark Twain's *Prince and the Pauper*? I failed that quiz, lying about having read it but just not understanding it. But by the time I hit junior high and then high school, I was introduced to better and better books, and my reading palette expanded, mixing genre and literary fiction. I read constantly, often late into the night. I always had a book with me. It was pure escapism, but also taught me a great deal, even if I wasn't conscious of it, about how language worked. And reading inspired me to try my own hand at writing. I sketched out fantasies, drawing the maps through which my characters would have their adventures, then writing out my stories longhand (no one had a computer or even a typewriter, though I wanted one, badly), double-spaced, on lined paper with red margin lines.

So, English as a major and teaching as a career combined a love of reading and writing with an attempt to control the situations — the classroom, the campus — that were often the site of my own torment. Just as I had played school, yielding the rod of correction over other kids, I planned to move into adulthood to enact those play fantasies for real. At the time, I couldn't have articulated these choices in this way. But I see now the deep, connected uncanniness of it all. Not that I regret any of it, much. I've managed to make something of a life out of escape and control, trying in adulthood to reverse the damages done by managing some of the scenes of torture. I can now inflict pain (if I want to, though I generally don't) in the spaces in which it was once inflicted on me. I can hold forth as a teacher and everyone will finally have to listen to me.

College offered something of a reprieve from bullying, with my fellow students probably both too overwhelmed by the size, complexity, and diversity of the campus and more focused on performing versions of potential adulthood. I welcomed the relief, though I remained quiet and reserved, rarely talking in class. One of my professors, in a letter of recommendation, even referred to me as "reticent," a word I had to look up, and one friend thought it might not be the very best modifier a teacher could use to describe someone in whom he had confidence.

I was only about ninety miles away at Louisiana State University in Baton Rouge, though I could've been on another planet. A huge, stately old campus, with large live oaks whose exposed root systems we were urged not to cut across for fear of damaging as we sought more expedient paths to class. After fleeing a crazy freshman roommate (he attacked me in my sleep because he thought I'd purposefully hidden his retainer), I moved into a room in a hundred-year-old former army barracks. No air-conditioning, though we could get a good breeze going with all the windows open. In the winter, which could see several days in a row in the 30s, we kept the windows open to balance out the radiator heating, which had only two settings: off and hell.

It was 1985 when I arrived at LSU, and I was free from both PE and religion classes. I was also around girls for the first real time. (I'd gone to my senior prom with a friend, who had somehow wrangled us both blind dates — so that didn't really count.) I almost immediately got some girlfriends, a couple who became more than just pals, and I thought in my heart that I had possibly found some salvation. They were often smart, deeply feeling, and interested in me. They were also girls, not boys, and I could all too easily read my interest in them — very likely more the shock of the new, a discovery of a whole new kind of humanity — as emerging proof that I wasn't going to be lost to the hells of homosexuality. Some of them were even a bit kinky. For my 19th birthday, I coaxed one of them into tying me to the bed and whipping my ass. I still remember that night fondly, perhaps thrilling now more to the trace memories of my sleek twink body than to the charms of Penny, who nonetheless often captivated me with her deep love of words and commitment to an aesthetic life. She also loved drinking and fooling around, and I caught on quickly to these two past times.

Indeed, one of the minor humiliations of aging is that I recall all too well the bodily sensations of being 19 and knowing now that my body will never feel that way again. I'd walk across the swelteringly humid Louisiana campus in a t-shirt and khaki shorts, and I think I could've pretty much fucked anything that would've let me. I'd orgasm multiple times a day, each time striving to feel a spasming in my middle toes, the ones between the big toe and the pinky. That quivering, an involuntary electric throbbing lasting seconds, signaled pure pleasure, a giving over of the body to carnal delight. I haven't felt that throbbing in nearly three decades.

For all of the orgasms, though, I wouldn't penetrate a young woman. Some begged, and I'm not bragging, really. Remember, it was 1985 when I arrived at LSU, and we were all watching Rock Hudson die on television; he actually passed away on October 2, the day I turned 18. In the deep south at the time, AIDS was so clearly understood as god's punishment for homosexuality (drug use, too) that I was practically scared straight. I'd fool around with the ladies, but no sex, even though sex with them would've seemed "safer" at the time. Indeed, the fear of AIDS, coupled with rampant homophobia, kept me fearful for both my soul and body.

And not all of the homophobia was vectored through organized religion. I remember going for my first AIDS test in the early '90s. I was starting a new relationship and was regretting—actually fearing for my life—my college-age fumblings with a young man. (More on this in a bit.) I sat in the clinic while the nurse drew blood. Another nurse inquired what test I was getting, shaking her head with disgust as my blood-letter told her: "That AIDS test." I had to call two weeks later to find out my test results, and when the nurse on the line looked at my chart, she said, "I'll have to let you talk to a doctor." She curtly put me on hold and I immediately stopped breathing. Even now, writing out this story, my breath shortens; I thought I was receiving a death sentence. The doctor came on the phone and told me that I was negative, everything was fine, and that only a doctor at the time could report such test results in Louisiana. I nearly sobbed with relief, and only later got angry: why couldn't the nurse have told me that a doctor would have to report the results? Her abrupt and dismissive comment—"I'll have to let you talk to a doctor"—seemed designed to punish me for even just seeking out the test. At the time, I was still indoctrinated enough into homophobic Christianity to believe I just might deserve such punishment, being the creep I was. In retrospect, the nurse's righteous dismissiveness seems its own brand of creepiness.

But what about those fumbling with another young man? Nice how I just slipped that in, thinking you might forget. But no, I have to confess: the true propulsions of my incipient creepiness came full throttle forward during my senior year. Let me set this up for you, for full effect.

As I said, besides my experiments with women, I'd kept pretty much under the radar sexually. Most weekends I'd go home to New Orleans, do some homework, go to church, and then take the bus back to campus. My explorations of homosexuality remained relatively theoretical. During my first-year honors biology course for humanities majors, for instance, I wrote a term paper about the origins of homosexuality, ultimately focusing more on the history of its denigration and steady rise to a kind of acceptance in the late twentieth century. I'd discovered John Boswell's *Christianity, Social Tolerance, and Homosexuality*, which had just come out five years earlier in 1980, and which passionately argued against homophobia, tracing tolerance for homosexuality to the early middle ages. As part of my "research," I convinced a group of friends to check out a local gay bar, and we even boldly went to a meeting of the gay student group on campus. The former experience was marked mostly by my horror at being cruised by a rather large older gay man (poor thing, he was probably only 30 and I bet he would have treated me well and gently). The latter proved more cautionary than enlightening as the group's discussion revolved mostly on in-fighting and bickering, with one graduate student, I believe, belittling his conversational opponent by suggesting he was anally receptive. Not the best put-down to combat internalized homophobia, I now realize. I walked away from both experiences more distressed than enthralled. So, my college years were fairly non-sexual, except for excessive masturbation and some limited kink with a couple of young women, although in time I would become a bit bolder as I moved toward 20, 21, feeling my adulthood emerging. But not before a brief non-affair with an older woman that likely propelled me forward into a tentative public probing of my queerness.

I had a group of older friends that I'd met through church, three musicians, Larry, his wife Jeanie, and the church pianist Faith. By older I mean they were in their 30s. I was totally taken with their interest in me and their willingness to spend time with me. We would all go out to eat, get season tickets to the New Orleans opera, exchange books, and generally enjoy each other's company. Larry, I remember with extraordinary fondness. He had a striking and powerful baritone, and I started composing music, little art songs based on the poetry I was reading, and he'd consent to sing them, even performing in church some of my arrangements of old hymns for solo voice. I spent many weekends overnight with them, and Faith and I eventually grew closer through our shared interest in the piano and indie film. She and I started seeing each other as friends outside this little group.

Lots of church drama ultimately drove Larry, Jeanie, and Faith from the church (something unfortunate about some members of the church not feeling comfortable with having a female minister of music, Jeanie), and the psychic toll on our little group was intense at times. I don't remember, and am not sure I ever fully knew, the nature of the tensions amongst my three older friends, but Faith and I saw more and more of each other separately. We'd head to uptown and watch foreign films at the Prytania, then browse the Maple Street Bookshop. I loved those Saturday afternoons. They seemed arty and smart. And they were. We'd even check out films that Jeanie frowned on us seeing, such as Merchant Ivory's adaptation of E.M. Forester's posthumously published *Maurice*, about a young man coming to terms with his homosexuality in Edwardian England. Did Faith suspect I was queer? I'm not sure but one weekend she drove to Baton Rouge to visit, and we had a delightful evening at a George Winston recital followed by pancakes at the IHOP before driving back to the city, where I crashed at her apartment (she sleeping on the couch). We never had sex, and at most would just hold one another. But I think she liked me, and I know I liked her, though I didn't think of her sexually. She eventually broke off our friendship and started dating in earnest people her own age. I was heartbroken. I didn't understand why we couldn't still be friends. Perhaps that was my limitation, perhaps hers, but it ended what had been a junior-year of relative happiness and stability, in which I felt wanted and admired by people I wanted to know and whom I admired.

I have to admit that I was a bit of a creep in the aftermath of the dissolution of my friendship with Faith. Not awfully so, but creepy nonetheless. I was so hurt that she wanted (really needed) to move on and that she wasn't going to continue to make room for me in her life. I wasn't in love with her, but, at 20 years of age, I was in love with her independence, her ability to lead her own life, her pursuit of her own interests, and even her decision to be decisive — the thing that hurt in terms of our relationship but that nonetheless seemed admirable. She knew what she wanted, and she went after it. And, of course, I was a bit in love with her interest in me, however muted, however modest, however much she knew I wasn't a reliable long-term object of romantic or sexual affection. In retrospect, I totally understand her decision, even if I think she could've been a little kinder about it.

And perhaps my inability to see in retrospect — again, I was 20 — prompted me one Sunday morning to show up at her church, where she sang in the choir, and just stare at her from my seat in the pews. I didn't approach her after church, I didn't warn her I was coming. I just showed up. And stared. I was creeping. I wanted her to know that she couldn't just discard me from her life, just kick me to the curb, just decide unilaterally that our friendship was done. But, of course, she could. And my showing up at her church to stare at her only spoke to my hurt and sense of betrayal. I was smart enough to realize that, and I didn't show up again.

But I wasn't mature enough yet to keep myself from other little acts of creepiness. A few months after not hearing from her and not reaching out myself, I called and we chatted for a bit. Our conversation was a bit awkward, but soon become friendly, almost like old times. I suggested we see a movie and we made a date, Faith actually seeming excited about getting together. But I was already planning to betray her. The night of our movie date, I was with Larry and Jeanie, her former friends. She called the house, and my mother told her that I was with them, reporting back to me later that Faith sounded hurt. My older self now is ashamed to admit that I was glad she was hurt. But hell, even my younger self at the time was a bit ashamed. This was just revenge, pure and simple. And whatever small satisfaction I got from inflicting pain was drowning in how small I felt. If I loved her, even just a friend, would I really want to hurt her like this?

Still, such questions couldn't quite prevent me from even little further bits of creepiness. I just couldn't quite stay away, not just yet. I prank called her a few times, just calling and hanging up as soon as she said hello. This was well before the time when it became incredibly easy to know who has called you, but I'm pretty sure Faith knew it was me. I called her once from Larry and Jeanie's house one evening, where I was staying the night, and within a minute of hanging up their phone rang a couple of times before stopping. I remember my face flushing and my friends wondering what was wrong. Of course, they had no idea, but I knew I'd been called out, my creepiness identified. I stopped calling and tried to forget about her. I mostly did and moved on, other dramas soon to take the place of this botched friendship.

And then, senior year. What the hell was I thinking? I was probably still psychically reeling from the dissolution of our little circle and my friendship with Faith. Or perhaps I was experiencing a late adolescent hormone surge. Or maybe the prospect of leaving college and really entering adulthood was scaring the shit out of me, as well as the other senior-level folks I was hanging out with. But I threw caution to the wind and unleashed a shitstorm in my life.

I joined the Student Union Film Committee, and that was the beginning of the problem. The Film Committee was run by the Student Government, which organized a variety of social and theme-driven groups and clubs. Our committee's primary charge was choosing the films that the Student Union would show in its dinky little theater: mostly indie films, but some blockbusters. I saw a lot of good movies. To this day, I remember my first viewing of *A Clockwork Orange* and Spalding Gray's *Swimming to Cambodia*. Walking out of the Kubrick film with a "girlfriend" in tow, I pompously began reciting in German Schiller's "Ode to Joy," which forms the text of Beethoven's final symphony's final movement's paean to brotherhood and which is used to great rhetorical and aesthetic effect in the film to ironize scenes of grotesque inhumanity. It's a truly creepy use of the music. My date was increasingly turned on by my precocity. What a little fucker I was, such a tease.

Anyway, enjoying film as I did it seemed like a good move socially to join this club. I'd meet some new people, perhaps some who would help me lick my Faith-inflicted wounds. And I did meet a group of smart, bright young folks, all pretty literary, some of whom I'd had classes with but didn't get to know in the midst of my relative anti-sociality. We met for the committee meetings and then would retire to the local college bars, the all-purpose Chimes or the smarty-pants Library or the skanky Bayou, and drink drink drink. Wow, I fucking loved to drink. At that time, we'd been grandfathered in, as Louisiana changed its legal drinking age to 21. So, I began the year at 20 fully intending to toxify my liver. And I'm sure I put a dent or two in it. We were all frequently lubricated, having mastered the arts of happy hour, drinking cheaply at 4, hitting the dining halls before they closed at 7, and then passing out, sometimes in each other's arms, relatively chastely, so we'd get a full night's sleep and be prepared for class the next day at 9. A good formula.

We even branded ourselves at one point, me creating a little poster: The New Decadence. It all felt good, like I'd found a home, at least a group to hang out with, a set with whom I could start to explore my preferences, my interests, my (dare I say) desires. I confessed my homoerotic interests, and so did some others. Two young women in the group, both previously straight, one dating a really cute and sweet boy, started making out one evening, and their affair began. Not to be left out, I started making out with the comic strip writer for the student newspaper, her bra winding up strewn across my bedside lamp. That image later appeared in a cartoon she published, inserting a can of Crisco next to the bed. (There was no Crisco in real life.) I remember opening the paper before class and yelping out loud, recognizing the scene, knowing this dorm room depicted was mine, and feeling I had "arrived" in some sense, that I was part of a scene, that I was a mover and a shaker, one whose exploits merited documentation, even dissemination, however coded and covert. And I hadn't even really had sex yet.

But despite however theoretical my homosexuality might have been, existing largely discursively, I tried to put theory and discourse to good use. I boldly proposed a film series, "Homosexuality in Film," typing up the rationale, listing such "classics" as *Making Love* and *The Boys in the Band*, photocopying my mini-manifesto, and distributing it at the meeting. I felt fucking badass. And, not to toot my horn too much, it was a bit daring. This was the '80s in the deep Deep South after all, and AIDS seemed to be announcing the wrath of god against queers everywhere. The chair, one of our little group, was supportive, although she didn't want people to know about her experimental sapphic affair. The proposal was outvoted by another, and I can't for the life of me remember what it was. Film Noir? No, nothing that smart. Maybe something chickenshit like Dance in Film. I was appalled by the small-mindedness of the world, my outrage resulting in several rounds of binge drinking as we all cried into our cocktails at The Chimes — the sapphic chair liked old fashioneds, I think, while I preferred something called Jet Fuel, which looked like Windex.

By that point, I'd already met in passing Matt S. He was on the film committee and an editorialist for the student newspaper, *The Daily Reveille* (which we lambasted as *The Daily Revile*). He was fucking gorgeous. Cleary intelligent, but also rakishly aware of his good looks, with a full head of luscious hair and piercing eyes oddly complementing his ever just so slightly pudgy body, which he paraded around campus in ratty shorts and a dirty t-shirt to intoxicating effect. He was loose and nonchalant, snarky and smart. I was completely smitten. He didn't know who the hell I was.

I began a complicated project of stalking. I found out that he lived in the same dorm complex as I did. I was in a ground floor suite in one building, he in an upper-floor suite two buildings over. I skulked around the old red-brick buildings day and night, hanging out in my own recently acquired nonchalance, totally studied and probably coming across more like barely controlled psychosis. I was (still am) a walker and a pacer, lapping multiple miles a day, either going to and fro destinations or just moving back and forth like a caged animal, patrolling the perimeters of my room. I must have circled the pentagon a thousand times, hoping for a glimpse of this boy. Then, as though fated, I saw him walking back from soccer practice with… my roommate, Nick, whose name wasn't really Nick but who called himself that because there's no conceivable way that most Louisianians could pronounce his Taiwanese name. I'd paid next to no attention to Nick, who was nice enough and whom I'd essentially just met earlier that term, poor thing being assigned a room at random with me. But now I was all over my roommate, asking him questions about Matt. Tell me about soccer! *Where do you play? Is this an official club? Oh, you know Matt? We're on the Film Committee together! I had no idea, really! Wow! We should all get a drink sometime!*

And we did, the three of us. And it was awful. Matt and I had clearly nothing in common, though we obviously did. We were both writers, of a sort, he a journalist and I a poet. Never did the genres of the language seem to erect such an insurmountable barrier, topped by glass shards and razor wire, electrified. We sipped our tepid beers while hunched around a sticky table stuck to the stickier floor of The Bayou, and I thought, "This is hell." His fat little hand gripping his beer just inches from my own as he flicked his hair out of his eyes taught me the meaning of the word swoon. Indeed, I'm sure the rancid odor of the bar couldn't overpower the scent of my attraction, and he consequently paid me little attention. Perhaps in those moments, even over and beyond my stalking around the dorm, my creepiness revealed itself. I couldn't take my eyes off him, but I had no idea what to say.

"You're a journalism major? I write poetry."
"I'm taking Sasek for Milton. I hate Milton."
"Milton is one of the best poets in the language."
"So Nick, nice goal yesterday…"

And with such verbal dexterity he sidelined me right out of the conversation, thrown summarily out of any Eden I might have been imagining as we sat hunched over those sticky tables.

As with any desire thwarted, a dream deferred, acute interest soon turned to active antagonism. My group of decadent friends knew all about my interest and some tried to dissuade me, correctly advising me that he wasn't right for me, not to mention that he couldn't care less about me. But some of them enjoyed the drunken sessions of prank phone calling we started. Late into the night, we'd call his room, hanging up, call, hang up, call hang up, call, hang up. To avoid too much repetition, we'd sometimes shout obscenities, masking our voices. I'm sure he knew we were calling him. He even called back once, the phone ringing after we'd just hung up, my sapphic friend whispering not to pick up, me unsure why she was whispering. I did, pretending I'd been roused from sleep. I don't think he was fooled, and he pretended he'd dialed the wrong number.

In a desperate move, I submitted an editorial to the student newspaper countering one of his. He'd written about how the Student Union should be willing, as an expression of free speech, to show not just indie films but also pornography. He was arguing particularly, I recall, for a showing of *Deep Throat*, calling it a groundbreaking film in the history of blue cinema. The part of me that still headed home some weekends and attended church was appalled. The id-driven strategist in me also saw an opportunity. Disgust and desire, often mirroring one another, resulted in my own editorial, which was published in response to his. That itself seemed like a victory. But what is truly strange is that I sincerely thought I could attract at least his attention by publicly attacking his interest in promoting free speech, however misguided his promotion was. (Fuck, by criticizing him even now I'm still trying to engage him.)

Was it still a surprise to me that he voted against my progressively ahead-of-its time proposal, "Homosexuality in Film"? Was it really? It was. His no still stung. Heavy rounds of drinking, and then more drinking and some awkward sexual fumbling with the girls, and then more drinking ensued. Sapphic chair had a car and, realizing that she was too drunk to drive us to our next location, she gave me her keys. I didn't have a driver's license and I was surely as fucked up as she. But I took the keys and we drove away into the night, me focusing on the white dashed lines to stay on the road while cars zipped around me. This madness played itself out not just once but twice, and I count it a miracle or sheer luck (still haven't decided) that I'm alive today, that she's alive today (at least according to Facebook, through which we have accepted "friendship" but never converse), that I didn't kill anyone else, and that I wasn't arrested and thrown under the jail. Why no one bothered to call the cops on us is also something of a mystery. On one of these jaunts, having peeled out of a bar's parking lot, we dizzyingly rolled into a K-Mart, stumbled to the fake jewelry counter, bought cheap gold-colored rings, declared ourselves married, and actually wore them for weeks, brandishing them at Film Committee meetings to show our alliance in defiance of the bigots and small-minded fuckers who opposed "Homosexuality in Film."

In those heady weeks, when I was trying to write an honors English thesis on the poetry of World War One, focusing on gay British poet Wilfred Owen and the mad Austrian Georg Trakl, I actually caught the attention of another member of the Film Committee, a tall slender gay guy my age, whose major I forget. He chatted me up once and I walked away thinking he was cute. But what next? I was still smitten with Matt S. What could I offer Mike W.? I mean, just even practically, I had no idea how to even go about asking a guy out on a date. I also didn't even know if he was into guys really. He seemed… gayish. But he wasn't particularly effeminate. And there are lots of guys who are into film and the arts. Hmmm. I had no models. I had only feelings and suspicions.

So, why not have him tag along, get him drunk, and see what happens? Drinking seemed to be the answer to everything, and given that I could apparently drive drunk with impunity, I felt fairly confident that through the bottle lay the path to pleasure, freedom from fear, and an approach to the kind of life I couldn't even really imagine but that I thought for sure would save me from the desperation I felt in the presence of Matt S. And sure enough, with enough alcohol, I turned from making out with the female cartoonist to making out with Mike W. I remember pulling away after we started kissing and saying, "You're scratchy." I'd never thought that even a clean-shaven guy's face would feel rough from stubble, not smooth like the girls I'd grown accustomed to kissing. But then I dived back in. We made out, fumbled around with each other, and then eventually fell asleep in each other's arms, while my other drunken friends sat around drinking and making out on their own, one of them saying, kindly, "I'm so happy for Jonathan."

To this day I remember that scene, that first kiss, that parting comment and my eyes brim with tears. I was 21.

It all fell apart within a few weeks, and rather dramatically. The drinking turned more desperate, even though I was now kissing a boy, perhaps *because* I was kissing a boy. The prank phone calls escalated. The second drunk driving escapade. It was ugly.

And then I got a phone call from the police. Someone had filed a complaint against me. I had to make an appointment to go talk to an officer, who gently read me my rights before asking me some questions. He asked if I was prank phone calling people. I denied it. He then asked about the Film Committee, and I explained about the film series I proposed and how, surely, the people who were accusing me of prank phone calling were just afraid of the ideas I was forwarding, of the waters I was testing. I knew how to hide, how to lie, even with half-truths. He listened patiently, and then explained that duly elected representatives to the Student Council had suggested that I was a dangerous and manipulative force, luring the unsuspected and once pristine into drunken depravity. My exploits were known and I needed to take care lest I jeopardize my entire future and become a complete creep. He referred the case to the Dean of Students, who warned me that the technology for tracing phone calls was getting better and better (as it was), and that that was something I should know whether or not I'd done anything wrong, whether or not I was being persecuted for being ahead of my time (my words, not his).

Writing this, I realize that the officer at the LSU police station was the first adult — as in not someone my age, not in college, but older and established as an adult — to whom I suggested I was gay. *A police officer.*

Was there no one else I could've talked to? Someone at my church? Someone in my family? My adult friends? Faith? It's hard at times not to think that, as creepy as I must have been and seemed, the surrounding situation was creepier still. There was no adult I felt I could safely talk to.

But my own creepinesss — my potential to destroy, not only myself but those around me — was what was on trial at the moment. My friends deserted me. I nearly lost my little part-time job teaching English as a second language to spoiled foreigners. And Mike broke up with me. He was both turned off by my drunken escapades, but also dissatisfied that all of our alcohol-fueled fumblings in bed had never actually resulted in orgasm. I'd suck, he'd suck — but nothing. We were all just too fucked up. And he wanted anal, and I just wasn't ready.

So, I ended my senior year, having nearly been arrested or thrown out of school, friendless and alone. I finished my thesis and graduated with honors. Then I moved back home for the summer, announcing that I was going to graduate school to study comparative literature. Despite having spent most of my last term in college inebriated, I'd gotten a teaching assistantship and full tuition remission at LSU, and I'd be amongst their first students in this new interdepartmental program. My parents were furious. They thought I'd move back home to teach English in the local high schools. To be fair, they just didn't understand what I was doing. From their perspective, I'd gone to college, and now it was time to get a job. But I intuited that, despite the last year's setbacks, there just had to be another world out there. And while everything else around me had let me down — or had punished me for stepping too far out of the norm — my books and writing hadn't. I'd stick with them. I'd stay where it was safe. And besides, fuck my parents. They hadn't paid for my college. I had to wait every single semester to see if a special scholarship would come through so I could afford to go. Some terms I wouldn't know until just days before classes started. And I'd be paying my way going forward, thanks to the generosity of the tax-paying bigots of Louisiana. How I mustered such defiance, I don't know. But there were a few days that summer that I spent in drunken stupor. And one incident with some tertiary friends in which, consuming screw drivers all the way up I-10 to a get-together in Baton Rouge (with someone else driving this time), I got to the party completely fucked up, passed out, and woke up the next morning to tales about how I'd tried to grab one of my guy friends. I didn't see much of these guys again.

All of these incidents scarred me, even if they didn't always scare me. I had tried to make a gay way in the world, without much guidance, with no mentor, lacking any positive role modeling, facing resistance and outright hostility, and stumbling my way through tortured feelings I didn't know how to manage or even fully understand, if we ever can understand the courses of desire. But I had tried, and I had failed. In no conceivable way could I "come out" to my parents. I felt shame about botching the job of trying to be gay, which only compounded the shame

I felt about being queer to begin with. Surely, god was sending me a powerful sign. *Don't go there. Homosexuality can lead to nothing good.* You need to remember that, at the time, in the mid-'80s, we didn't have the relative plethora of relatively sane images of gays and lesbians on television and in the movies that we do now. Not only were queers, associated with drug users and prostitutes, part of the media spectacle of AIDS, but countervailing narratives of gay pride were hard to find in the Deep South of the Reagan years. I can't recall one positive representation of a gay man from television. I remember a brief, short-lived series, "Love, Sidney," with Tony Randall, who played a lonely old gay man, his younger lover having left or died, I can't remember which. The prospects didn't seem good for sustainable queerness. But surely, you're thinking, you were near New Orleans, you must have had some access to queerness? But no. I knew no gay adults (with one exception, which I'll get to later). I suspected that some of my teachers, both in high school and in college, might be gay, but no one was out. How I ever thought that I could come out as a teacher, which I eventually did, still surprises me.

In graduate school, having returned to dating young women, and turning my attention in particular to a smart fellow New Orleanian I would eventually marry, I sought counseling to contend with my feelings of shame and despair. I wanted to try to cure the inner creep. By that point, I was telling myself a complicated narrative: all of the homophobic slurs that were used to bully me as a child had left me feeling that I, in fact, might actually be queer. Perhaps my sexuality had been detoured from its just, true, and straight path. Perhaps I couldn't make a go of being gay because I wasn't *really* gay. Indeed, to this day, I can't tell if I like men because of some deep-seated predisposition or if, over several formative years of puberty by being labeled, constantly, insistently, irrevocably, I eventually just psychically gave in to the ceaseless interpellation. At this point in my life, I don't know that I care. The etiology of my desires is less interesting than the complexity of strategizing for their fulfillment. But the genealogy of my creepiness fascinates — now. At the time, though, it was just horrifying. I was a young man suffering from years of abuse. Is there any wonder then that I found myself a couple of times sitting alone late at night in a bathtub of tepid water considering how I might slit my wrists?

Fearing such thoughts and thinking that I should give god another chance, I found a Christian counselor who readily supported my interpretation that I'd been bullied into thinking myself queer, and he gently advised me to continue praying about the issues. God would understand. I'd been tested and tempted, but seeking help was the right thing to do. I want to be fair here: this wasn't conversion therapy. I believe this man was genuinely concerned about me — as he damn well should have been, given the amount of bullying and abuse I'd suffered as a child. And his pre-ordained response — to encourage a healthy heterosexuality as opposed to a heinous homosexuality — is totally understandable given the time and the area. But it also vectored a powerful emotional solution: "God will give you a son." That was his answer. He was convinced that god would provide me a boy of my own to raise and love, and that that would be healing in ways I couldn't even imagine. To this day, I'm moved by this gesture to comfort, to prophecy in the name of healing, to provide a solace that recognized my need for some human warmth from a male. He believed, as I wanted terribly to believe myself, that having a son would allow me to experience myself as a caring father, and eventually a friend, that I never had in my own father, and that I rarely found in male friends.

No, god never gave me a son. I will admit that I never tried that hard to have one. Not that there wasn't possibility; I was after all married to a woman for a while. But even then, something in me balked against having my own child. Some deep-down instinct said no, let's stop the madness, let's refuse to pass on this genetic material, let's end the line with me. It's as though, in cutting off the possibility of my having a child, I would prevent further abuse. When my wife wanted to go on Norplant, I readily supported the decision.

Indeed, about my wife. I got married to a wonderful young woman; we were together for several years, finishing graduate school, leaving Louisiana and moving to Colorado to set up a life together away from all we had known and all that had made us suffer in our youth. Her story needs a book of its own, and I respect her enough to let her tell her own story. Suffice it to say that we were smart enough after three years of marriage to recognize that, while we needed each other to get out of the south, we didn't need each other to craft sustainable and fulfilling adulthoods. We might even have started to hold each other back if we hadn't parted as husband and wife.

So, we divorced right around the time I came out as queer, started developing a new friendship circle, turned my attention to writing actively about queerness, began teaching courses in queer theory and LGBT studies, started dating men (three at one time even!), found my current partner, refocused energy on my career, started publishing a range of work, moved up the academic ladder, got married to a man, etc., etc. I'm obviously skipping over a lot, but there's a way in which the last twenty years of my life — as eventful as they have been, and as deserving of their own story as they are (if only I thought that anyone cared to read about it) — have been an attempt to deal with that first twenty years, to make a survivable, much less enjoyable, life out of the damages foregoing. I have not always been successful, even though external markers suggest otherwise. Indeed, it's precisely that disconnect — visibly living a successful life while mostly feeling like shit, and periodically avoiding, just narrowly, my best efforts to sabotage my life — that remains the truest, most persistent legacy of my youth. And it's the feeling like shit, and the sabotage, that comes straight out of my own deep down feeling of creepiness, the sheer weirdness I carry with me, the substantial strangeness that animates nearly everything I do, how I experience the world.

When younger, I would stage for myself triumphal returns, such as a couple of lectures at LSU that I talked former professors into offering me. I would strut on campus, walking amongst the stately old live oaks, looking on past sites of youthful self-degradation and feel myself not only a survivor but even victorious. *Look what I've done. Look at me now.* I remember walking into a former professor's office, someone I really adored as a young man but whom I hadn't seen in years, nearly two decades. "You're so… big," he said. And I was. Fatter, surely. But a college friend of mine remarked that, as tall as I was, I was often stooped, bent in on myself as a young person, afraid, meek. Now I stood tall. I'm not sure I felt tall, but I had learned to fake it well. I might be successful, even openly gay now, but deep down, I was still a creep.

A Theory

"All of us who survived those common years had to be a little strange."
—Audre Lorde

If I move now from the particulars of my childhood and youth to something called "theory," I do so only because theory—plotting out, thematizing, making schematic, and abstracting a set of experiences into some general impressions of a way of being in the world—has been one way I have tried to survive myself. Making something abstract is a way to understand it, and understanding brings, if not control, at least coping. The impulse to theorize caters to the desire to organize the mess. It's a powerful form of pattern recognition. It's our need for truth. So here I theorize my creepiness, pulling from my personal narrative more particular moments that deserve critical attention, an interpretive gaze that might help me understand better the genealogy of how I have either come to understand myself as creepy, how others have at times identified me as a creep, or both.

Ultimately, I'm not sure what truth I can make out of creepiness, but in working my experiences through a word—a word with significant resonances in our culture at the moment—we might learn something about how the larger culture normalizes and stigmatizes certain ways of moving in the world. What are those resonances? Creepiness isn't an official psychological category, but, as we've noted, it's widely deployed in a variety of ways to mark the emotionally messy, a certain covertness of desire, a lingering inappropriateness of interest. It's that which doesn't belong but somehow sticks around. Think for instance of the classic song of self-identified creepiness, Radiohead's "Creep."

The lyrics gesture simultaneously to the individual creep's self-absorption — "I want a perfect body, I want a perfect soul, I wish I was special" — and to his overwrought attachment to an object of desire — "You're so fucking special [...] whatever you want." At the same time, the creep also has self-consciousness; this creep asks, "What the hell am I doing here?," and he can only respond by admitting, "I don't belong here."[1]

Speaking personally, I've spent way too much time listening to this song and tearing up over some boy who just wouldn't love me. I say that, thinking I'm pathetic, knowing that I enjoyed the emotional self-flagellation, relishing masochistically the identification with the creep, the one who wants control, the perfect soul, but who is still cast aside, who doesn't belong. Maybe some of us have to fetishize our outsider status. If you can't beat them, after all... But the popularity of the song, and its ability to resurface throughout the years in multiple covers and in various media, suggests that many of us identify with both that outsiderness as well as the sense that, at times, we have perhaps lingered just a little bit too long, making ourselves unwelcome, our outsiderness uncomfortable not just for ourselves but for others as well.

Adam Kotsko is amongst the few theorists and commentators who tackles the fascination of the creep head on. The author previously of a provocatively titled book, *Why We Love Sociopaths*, Kotsko undertakes in his more recent volume, *Creepiness*, an examination of the figure of the creep throughout a variety of movie and televisual examples, ranging from Jim Carrey's obsessed and menacing *Cable Guy*, to the strange rictus face of the Burger King, who weirdly appears in a guy's bed as he's contemplating a meal choice, to the high and tortured drama of *Mad*

1 My favorite version of this is Chrissie Hynde and The Pretenders' moving cover, "Creep by The Pretenders," YouTube video, 3:50, posted by Luciano Werhli, May 4, 2007, https://www.youtube.com/watch?v=lML2N4xB9GU. Many other versions and covers abound on the Internet.

Men's Don Draper, and the overall creeping of advertising into all aspects of American life.[2] The variety of creeps is astonishing, to say the least, but Kotsko returns frequently to the figure of the "creepy uncle" as a particularly potent "cultural trope," one that many of us readily recognize. Why? For Kotsko, the "creepy uncle" is creepy in that he occupies a liminal space, his position not quite defined in traditional family structures. As Kotsko puts it, "It is the uncle's displaced and enigmatic role as 'family but not *really* family' that opens up the space for other creepy tropes to attach to the figure of the uncle in a way that is not really possible for a more clearly defined role like that of the father."[3] That creepy uncle is part of the family, surely, but not part of the central group, so his intentions are potentially suspect, his interest in the family questionable. At the very least, he represents alternative models or possibilities of adulthood for children in the central family, perhaps alternatives that diverge from the primary family's investment in its children. Sometimes the uncle's interest in a family's children is coded as sexual as a way to mark it as dangerous or unwanted. Indeed, Kotsko's approach is pretty Freudian, and he identifies creepiness as emerging through "unmanageable" and "unruly desires" that threaten the "patriarchal nuclear families where any sexual indulgence outside the boundaries of heterosexual marriage was considered destructive and shameful."[4] To be sure, Kotsko's aim is not so much to *defend* those patriarchal nuclear families, or what he also calls the "traditional American family," but rather to trace how creepiness emerges structurally in relation to the power of the family as a primary unit and source of cultural and personal meaning.

Creeps aren't always just uncles, even if they are often situated adjacently to primary family units. One of Kotsko's favorite examples is Steve Urkel from the sitcom *Family Matters*. Steve, a

2 Adam Kotsko, *Creepiness* (Winchester: Zero Books, 2015).

3 Ibid., 12.

4 Ibid., 20.

gangly and bespectacled teen nerd, is always barging in on a traditional family trying to cope with its day-to-day suburban existence: "He is invasive, constantly dropping in on his neighbors unannounced. His desire is both enigmatic and excessive."[5] He's particularly fascinated by the family's teen daughter, though it's clear she's completely uninterested. In fact, the entire family isn't much interested in this kid, who is clearly trying to glom onto this more "normal" family as a way to compensate for the deficiencies in his own. In this way, for Kotsko at least, part of Urkel's creepiness lies in his calling attention to the fact that not all families are, indeed, normal and traditional, and that the structures that give legitimacy to us are not only capable of breaking down but are perhaps extremely fragile.

Even more curiously, though, Urkel isn't a minor character in *Family Matters,* and in many ways, he becomes the real star and focus of the show. His creepiness fascinates in part not just because it speaks to underlying anxieties about the fragility of family structures but also because it gestures to alternative possibilities for relationality. There are other ways of getting along and forming family, however strange, and if your family is somehow deficient, you can try to form your own. Ultimately, as Kotsko puts it, "[h]ere creepiness is not something to be shunned or hidden, but a source of profound power and liberation."[6] Herein lies Kotsko's most interesting theorizing about creepiness, which almost raises the specter of the creep to the level of critical insight. For Kotsko, "[c]reepiness points toward the ultimate breakdown of the social order at the same time as it accounts for its origin and its present hold on its members. Creepiness is thus the past, present, and future of human society: its eternal precondition, its eternal motor, and its eternal obstacle."[7] That's a sentence somewhat creepy in its own excess, its "eternal" overstatement of the case. But I take the force of his comment: we use the label

5 Ibid., 25.
6 Ibid., 48.
7 Ibid., 121.

of creepiness both to discipline others and to maintain norms of relationality, while the specter of the creep constantly points out the excesses of desire itself, and the always present possibilities for other ways of vectoring our desires into different forms of sociality. Urkel, that is, creeps us out a bit because he shows us that there are other ways to make family. Thus, his creepiness is inevitably somewhat sexual in that the traditional family revolves around — is indeed based on — sexual and intimate ties. As such, as Kotsko puts it, creepiness is fascinating "because it is fundamentally about our struggle with desire and sexuality."[8] Sexuality that exceeds the norms of the family gestures to alternatives that potentially threaten that family, or provide at least tempting alternatives to it — making the figure of the creep not just someone who threatens from outside the family but also potentially from within it: "We are susceptible to being creeped out [...] because we are always in danger of being creeped out by ourselves, or more precisely, by those parts of ourselves that seem to exceed and elude us."[9] Creepy uncles were once members of their own nuclear families, after all.

If all of this sounds vaguely Freudian, well, it is. Kotsko relies at times on psychoanalytic models, which makes sense given his focus on the creep in relation to traditional family structures. Indeed, Freud's concept related to creepiness, the "uncanny," is actually rooted in a discussion of what lies in and *outside* the home — the "unheimlich."[10] In scholarly fashion, Freud's meditation on the uncanny begins with an attempt to differentiate his views from previous commentators, particularly one E. Jentsch, but he also drawn on various literary sources, especially the work of E.T.A. Hoffman and his mechanical doll in the story

8 Ibid., 14.

9 Ibid.

10 All quotations from Freud and his essay on "The 'Uncanny'" are taken from the following: Sigmund Freud, "The 'Uncanny,'" trans. Alix Strachey, in *On Creativity and the Unconscious: Papers on the Psychology of Art, Literature, Love, Religions,* selected by Benjamin Nelson (New York: Harper Colophon, 1958). "The 'Uncanny'" was first published in Imago in 1919.

of "The Sand Man," which Jentsch himself had made much of in describing the experience of the uncanny. And indeed, the term the "uncanny valley" has come to describe the uneasy and creepy sensations people experience when encountering robots that seem a bit too life-like. But while acknowledging the usefulness of Jentsch's thoughts, Freud's interests lie slightly elsewhere, and he undertakes an analysis of the different possible origins of the word "unheimlich," which he notes is "obviously the opposite of *heimlich, heimisch*, meaning 'familiar'; 'native,' 'belonging to the home.'"[11] Of course, the analyst most concerned with traumatic family romances and early childhood fears of castration would be drawn to understanding the origin of the feeling of the uncanny, the *unheimlich*, as grounded in an unsettling experience of home. And indeed, it's not long before Freud is theorizing that the "uncanny is in reality nothing new or foreign, but something familiar and old-established in the mind that has been estranged only by the process of repression."[12] Ah, repression; what phenomenon of psyche can't be explained by (or blamed on) repression? Freud explains:

> There is a humorous saying: "Love is home-sickness"; and whenever a man dreams of a place or a country and says to himself, still in the dream, "this place is familiar to me, I have been there before," we may interpret the place as being his mother's genitals or her body. In this case, too, the *unheimlich* is what was once heimisch, home-like, familiar; the prefix "un" is the token of repression.[13]

Reading this I'm struck both by the power of the interpretive matrix here, something akin to an algorithm that generates patterns out of varied data inputs, and by Freud's fairly consistent fascination, creepy in its own way, with children and their relationship to adult genitalia.

---

11 Ibid., 124.
12 Ibid., 148.
13 Ibid., 153.

Of course, Freud has to admit that not everything repressed returns with the sensation of the uncanny, and he broadens out his theorization to include two types of uncanniness: "An uncanny experience occurs either when repressed infantile complex have been revived by some impression, or when the primitive beliefs we have surmounted seem once more to be confirmed."[14] This second kind of uncanniness occurs when, say, you were just thinking of someone and then—poof!—there they are, as though your thoughts have called them forth. It's the experience of the world as magical, full of coincidences not rationally explained. Such a sense of magic, Freud asserts, used to dominate our thinking before the rise of reason, science, and rational thought began chipping away at the edifices of superstition and religion. But vestiges of such magical thinking remain, just like the psychic leftovers of infantile sexual complexes, and they emerge at times to make the world around us strange and creepy.

Beyond the superstitious, I'm unsure how far down Freud's various rabbit holes (oops, an unconscious reference to my mother's genitalia?) I want to go, but I *am* moved by his insight that the "uncanny is in reality nothing new or foreign, but something familiar and old-established in the mind that has been estranged only by the process of repression." And Freud's interest in rooting such estrangement in the *home*—the *Heim*—seems right to me. For many of us creeps, something happens in the home, or close to it, that estranges us from ourselves, and from others. We become *other,* discovering our own fundamental weirdness, catching glimpses of it initially in how strangely family and potential friends react to us. I think of the things that my own family and neighbors reacted to, sometimes trying to correct—a bit of effeminacy here, a shyness there, or my crossed-eyes, my overly large head. Such outward signs seemed to speak of something potentially amiss internally, some deep-down flaw

14 Ibid., 157.

that made me not quite recognizable as a normal child, or even sometimes as fully human.

I might differ with Freud on the nature of repression, which may or may not be a coping function for dealing with infantile sexuality. Repression sometimes comes in blunter forms: my mother batting my hand away from sweeping my hair out of my eyes "like a girl"; a father wondering if I'm his child; other adults not letting their children play with the weird-looking kid; the constant taunts from other children who ruthlessly (if ultimately accurately) identified me as a faggot. How could such forces of repression — generally understood at the time as normal childhood teasing or adult attempts to correct undesirable behavior — not estrange me from myself, making me all the more inward-facing, introverted, self-doubting? Or worse, *self-hating*? Surely, there was a lot of material to work with, large-headed and crossed-eyed as I was (and remain). Even now I want to make excuses for those who abused me because I so long ago, at such an early age, began internalizing their sense that I was a creepy little kid who was, justly, the object of childhood scorn and adult skepticism.

My uncanniness — to others and to myself — did indeed start at home. I was *un-homed*, as it were, in many ways. I cannot deny that I've come a long way, baby, having built a successful career and a fairly stable life with my husband. But my sense of being an outsider remains. I struggle with the notion of home, of feeling at home. My professional life has not exactly been itinerant, but I'm only just now, approaching 50, allowing myself the possibility of staying in one place for more than a decade. I've otherwise moved around a lot, and I feel I'm perpetually looking for another job, another teaching position in another part of the country that might feel more like home. I've tried out several places after fleeing the south: first Colorado, then the Midwest, now California, but I've also spent huge chunks of time in the northeast, wondering if, perhaps, I might feel at home there. I don't know quite where I'll wind up at times, and my recurring paranoid fantasy is of *homelessness*, of being found one day dead on the streets of some other city, having lost everything, abandoned by everyone, abandoning myself finally and materially to the homelessness I've always felt deep down.

Such thoughts have prompted me to consider what alternative kinds of family life might have been possible for me to imagine at an earlier age. Like Steve Urkel, how might I have tried to construct another kind of home for myself, at least in my mind? Or is such imagination of alternative family even possible for a child? Is imagining another home only possible in adulthood? I recently got a sense of such imaginative possibilities when visiting with extended family, when I was reminded that, perhaps unsurprisingly, the most significant potential creep in my young life was my uncle, my mother's brother.

Hot and humid, unsurprisingly, when I land at the Gulfport International Airport in June 2014 to visit my mother. Every summer I spend about two weeks with her. She's 70, still works, remains in decent health, perhaps too ornery and spirited to slow down, though I can tell she wants to. But her Cajun blood runs warm, and since my father passed about a decade ago from Parkinson's disease, in the awful aftermath of Katrina, she's found new energies and interests in her life after caretaking. I'm happy for her. She's a bit alone at times in her small retirement home on the Mississippi Gulf Coast, having fled the City That Care Forgot some years ago, but close enough to my sister and her family not to feel lonely.

Still, I know she misses her siblings. Coming from a family of eight, there are only three of them left. And southern Mississippi just isn't "home." So I'm not surprised that she asked this summer to drive a bit over three hundred miles, clear across Louisiana, to visit her remaining (older) sister and (younger) brother in far west Louisiana, near Lake Charles. Cajun country.

My aunt, uncle, and cousins live, if not exactly in the bayous, pretty damn close to them. They've made their homes in trailers, some of them building houses, in the sticky wet heat, many of them working on the oil rigs in the Gulf and in neighboring Texas, all of them trying to get together as often as they can for family time, large gatherings of generally good cheer, drinking, and gossip.

My cousins prepared us just such a get-together to celebrate our visit. Smoked meats and barbecued chicken, Andouille sausage, boiled crawfish and boudin, the white sausage Cajuns love. We arrived one evening and ate our way through the next day, as twenty, thirty people stopped by for food and fellowship.

I was glad to see my cousins. I hadn't known many of them as a child; visits with my mother's large family were infrequent. In their early twenties, my mother and her brother Glen had moved away from Cajun country to try out life in the "big city," New Orleans — where they both stayed and made their lives and where my mother had me and my sisters. In early adulthood, they had relied on each other and a change of venue to remake their lives. Both black sheep — he gay, she a little too loud for a woman — both wanting to get away from an alcoholic and, at times, abusive father. Brighter lights beckoned.

As children, my sister and I saw a lot of my uncle, but my mother's other siblings and their children were hundreds of miles away, so my sisters and I got to know them only intermittently. It was only in the aftermath of Katrina that I connected with some of them in very moving ways. I'd flown down to stay with my mother and father, soon to pass, as they evacuated from the Mississippi Gulf Coast to Lake Charles. In those weeks, especially after my father's death (his body just couldn't stand the strain of the evacuation, having lived with Parkinson's for well over a decade — more on this later), I got to know this part of my family — their strength, their generosity, their care for one another. Good people. They were kind to my mother in her time of loss, sheltering her and grieving with her. I remain in their debt.

This visit, nearly a decade later, was a chance to reconnect, but also to grieve anew, as one of my aunts had just passed about seven months previously. Aunt Put, we called her. Like my mother, a feisty character, larger than life. She'd been the postmistress in her community, and she hated the word postmistress. She was the post*master*. I felt for my cousin's loss, even as I felt estranged still, this particular aunt disproving of homosexuality.

So, this gathering both celebrated our reunion and marked the transitions of time through which we all try to make our lives. That marking took a particular form as my mother, uncle, aunt, and their families sat around my cousin's kitchen island, sifting through hundreds and hundreds of photographs that my aunt had taken and collected. There may have been a thousand pictures — boxes of them. My cousins wanted to label them, calling on my mother's generation to identify people they didn't know. So, in between bouts of eating slow-cooked and spicy food, everyone sifted through the photographs, some eighty years old, scrutinizing the past and remembering lives lived and lost. Some faces and scenes remained opaque to memory. But many others evoked fondness and commiseration, and a couple of them a sense of the damage wrought by people on each other — even people who love one another. Several were pictures of family members in uniform, from World War II or the Korean War. Some were on oil rigs. Many were from family reunions. We organized the pictures primarily by closest association with my aunts and uncles. Eight large plastic baggies slowly accumulated the networks of relations, sorting memories through family ties, blood connections, and miscellaneous friendships.

At one point, a few of my relatives turned to me with a baggie full of photos of my uncle Glen, the one who had moved with my mother to New Orleans early in their adulthoods. With the baggie was a deathbook, the bound volume that guests at a wake sign so the family can have a memento of who mourned with them. My uncle, the one I'd known the best through sheer proximity to us in New Orleans, had died of multiple myeloma cancer when I was a sophomore in high school. My cousin, whose house hosted the gathering, whose mother had passed a half-year ago, and who was organizing the event, said that I should take the book and whatever pictures I wanted. Others around the table agreed, shaking their heads somberly. This seemed right. I had known him, after all, in ways I hadn't known anyone else in my mother's family.

He was also, like I am, gay.

In the moments after this gifting, I felt a welter of emotions. Part of me was extraordinarily touched by the gesture. It was such a thoughtful recognition of my past relationship with my uncle. Another part of me, though, felt that this handing off to me of his deathbook and photos was a simultaneous acknowledgment and disavowal of our shared queerness. The identity was recognized, but the gift also seemed to say, "This is your thing. It really belongs to you, not us." Perhaps the fact that only one — only one — of my cousins asked me about Mack, my husband and partner of nearly two decades, prompted me to feel that my queerness, along with Glen's, was being both evoked and dismissed at the same time. We were family, but also somehow not.

Indeed, Glen had left rural Louisiana, not finding it possible to make a life there as a gay man. I, in my own turn, had left Louisiana behind as well. We had both become "outsiders" to our families of origin, our shared extended family not exactly throwing us out, as is the case with many other queers, but still not fully comfortable with us either. We had both been raised to understand our queerness as a problem, even damning to our eternal souls. At best, socially shameful and creepy; at worst, an ungodly disgrace. And while my relatives might indulge a familial sense that we are "their" queers, we are still queers. At the reunion, I walked into a room where distant cousins were talking about the "freaks" they'd seen on a trip to San Francisco; everyone quickly shut up — embarrassed, surely, and not wanting to offend, but also annoyed that I'd interrupted their bonding. To be sure, at this point in my life, late 40s, comfortable with myself and largely at ease in my queer flesh, I have fewer and fewer family-oriented resentments. But I also know that I had to leave; like my uncle, I needed — and need still — a different set of relations.

At the same time, these people are my relations, my family, however uncanny — *unheimlich* — we might seem to one another. And this moment has provoked me to think about the genealogies that exist, both overtly and covertly, in any family. For while I may have strayed from both my immediate and extended families in many ways, the gifting of Glen's memorabilia makes visible to me alternative genealogies, different trajectories of affiliation, divergent paths of contact and influence — paths that even my family, so clearly ill at ease with queerness, could acknowledge.

Those genealogies orient us queerly to other ways of being — within and without — a sense of "family." What's perhaps most moving, most poignant for me, is that I knew my uncle for such a short period of time; he passed away right as I was entering adolescence. Yet his influence on my life has been profound. And however phantasmic my relatives' understanding of that relationship — queer uncle, queer nephew: they must somehow be "related" — my uncle's life and then his death, even thirty years later, is about lost trajectories, an only ever-guessed lost futurity that, in ways known and unknowable to me, I have spent most of my life trying to construct.

As kids, my sister and I thought nothing of Uncle Glen coming over to visit with his partner, Michael. They were just Glen and Michael, bringing beignets to eat on Sunday mornings. Other times, we'd visit them at their home in the French Quarter, an amazing shotgun where they had dinner parties, a bedroom ceiling draped with sheets and white Christmas lights like a fairyland, a back garden for drinking wine, a stereo tinkling out Tomita's synthesized classics. Aesthetic culture was important to them, I connected with my uncle through classical music and reading, mostly fantasy, C.S. Lewis and J.R.R. Tolkien. When I was eight, Uncle Glen took me to see *Fantasia*, and that experience alone probably did more to shape my future interest in the fantastical, the power of the imagination, fine music, and animation — interests that abide with me, sustain me, and, in so many ways, direct my ongoing investments, personally and professionally.

One Halloween they brought a stunning black costume for me, headpiece and all, literally a set of drapes that wrapped around my body, inlaid with little bits of mirror. I wanted to be Darth Vader but looked instead like an evil drag queen, glorious in my gowns. My parents wouldn't let me wear it — too over the top, too *creepy*. But to this day, I thrill to my uncle and his partner's boldness, their audacity, their sheer queer fabulousness. I loved them, both of them. For Glen's funeral, I would compose and play an elegy on the organ.

But childhood ends, and it ended for me abruptly with the hurt look on my uncle's face when I told a homophobic story I'd heard in school one day in late October. I was a ninth grader at the local Catholic boys' school, where my mother later hoped I'd one day return to teach, buying a home down the road from their house, just like some of her sibling's children did to stay close to their parents. The health teacher had told us about a friend of his who worked in the emergency room of a local hospital, about the faggots who would come in at night, having stuck things up their asses. Once, as the teacher's friend probed a guy's rectum, he saw a light looking back at him, a flashlight that the queer had stuck up his rear to pleasure himself. We boys laughed, squirming in our hard seats with titillated horror. I shared the story, and my uncle flew into a rage as he sewed our Halloween costumes that year. Already dying of cancer (he'd be dead within a half year), he rightly shouted that he didn't need to know about other people's problems, having enough of his own. My mother took me aside later and said, "Don't you know he's one of them?" I knew immediately what she was talking about. I'd had no idea, consciously.

Part of me wants to feel shame about this story, to feel that I hurt a fellow traveler, my own uncle. But, at thirteen, I was starting to figure out how to pleasure myself but hadn't yet connected the varieties of pleasure to particular identities. The story about the flashlight seemed, well, funny. A guy sticking a flashlight up his ass. That's funny to a thirteen-year-old boy. Not sexual, or at least it wasn't to me at the time. But the teacher (may he rot in hell, I still tell myself) was old enough to link the practice with an identity. I see now that he was training us. *You do shit like this and you're an object of scorn, deserving humiliating laughter at best, or even disciplining violence.*

Isn't the telling of this story to a room full of thirteen-year-old boys what's *really* creepy here?

I lost something that day—an innocence, surely, and began feeling the workings of social power in my own body, vectoring through the joke and rebounding on me in self-doubt and anxiety. I had offended, but my uncle was already himself, in his sexuality, offensive. I just hadn't known it. Now I did, and I realized that I might be an offender as well, if I didn't watch out.

And here, one strain of this narrative ends. Later that same school year, in just a few months, my uncle was dead—shortly after Mardi Gras. I remember my mother going to pick him up in the French Quarter on Mardi Gras night, because he had been abandoned by friends who wanted to go partying. He was just too weak. As she brought him home and led him to bed; he stopped by my room where I was just starting to listen to Aaron Copland's "Appalachian Spring." He asked if he could listen for a moment. It was our last meaningful exchange.

Or perhaps not. The dead often stay with us. And while it took me well over another decade to come out, I thought of my uncle all the time. I still do. But mostly what I think about is how my life might have been different had he survived. What would my adolescence have been like with him in it? Would it have been easier to come out, or harder? Would I have felt the need to distance myself from him in order to protect myself? Or might I have come out much earlier?

Although he was taken out of my life so early, my uncle haunted me — in good and bad ways — for a long time. For my family, he became the cautionary tale. Look what happens to those poor queers, dead so young. He was only 41. And some even speculated — and do so to this day — that his cancer might have been a mistaken diagnosis for AIDS. You don't want to be like him. Such words resonated with the hostility of the health teacher, and I sometimes vowed to myself not to be like my uncle. And yet his fabulous home in the French Quarter, his love of music and costuming, his delight in food, his boldness in bringing over his lover — all were also part of my life, gesturing, pointing, orienting me toward paths beyond the cautionary, the safe routes. As such, they formed part of an alternative genealogy, one that lay alongside, however hidden at times, the genealogical imperative that I satisfy certain familial demands and obligations — that I buy a home near my family, get married, get to work, and take care of my parents as they once took care of me.

I will never know what my uncle's presence might have made possible or imaginable had he survived. But I am nonetheless left with those foreclosed-upon possibilities, those unknowable trajectories. Indeed, what seems important to me now is marking both the place in my life that my uncle occupied while he was alive and marking what his absence throughout my adolescence actually did. I could've had a gay guide — a gay "dad" in my uncle. In this light, what my uncle's survival might have meant for me was a local modeling of a working-class queer man making queerness livable — if not in fact absolutely fabulous. What's at stake here is proximity. And what his death meant for me was a foreclosing of possibilities, at least possibilities for imagining a queer life in New Orleans.

That foreclosing meant that I stayed in an intensely homophobic environment. I knew no other adult who was gay or lesbian — for the remainder of my time in Louisiana, where I stayed until I was twenty-five. No one. Not one teacher, not one supervisor, certainly not a member of any church I attended. Looking back, I can't blame them; what a toxic place and time to be queer. And while I met some other young men, just a handful, like Mike W., they were often like me grappling with the damaging effects of homophobia on their own lives, so they couldn't help me any more than they could help themselves. We tried at times, as I've recounted. But it wasn't enough.

And it certainly wasn't enough to prevent me from wondering, in my early 20s, if my own homoerotic feelings might have stemmed from my uncle — not genetically, but because he may have sexually abused me as a child. I slowly began to build this narrative of his own creepiness, how he was very likely a sexual predator, and that everything wrong with my life I could lay at his feet. I fetishized particular memories to piece this story together. Once, I must have been may be 4 or 5, my uncle visiting us, my mother cooking in the kitchen, me cavorting around in my briefs, my uncle dropped an ice cube down the back of my tighty-whities. I remember screaming with outraged delight, but in my 20s, such a memory became a piece in a larger puzzle of predation and abuse. I couldn't remember anything else, but isn't the failure to remember itself a clue to possible abuse? I'd been reading Freud and thought I knew all about repression.

When, shortly before I got married to a woman, I broke down from the stress of it all and sobbed in my parents' kitchen. My mother didn't know what was going on, but my father said, in words I think I can recall perfectly: "I think I know what's wrong. You're a homosexual." I stopped crying and actually laughed. My reply haunts me to this day: "Well you're partly right. I think Uncle Glen abused me." I spilled out my concocted story, and my parents seemed all too eager to corroborate. There was that time, Glen having taken me to see *Fantasia* so my parents could go out for the evening themselves. Again, I must have been barely 5 or 6. I vaguely recall the film, not much else. After the movie, I'd apparently asked to call home and begged my parents to come get me. They didn't, still enjoying some time alone. And that must have been when it occurred, one of the instances of "abuse." Surely my pleas to go home signaled a distress that my parents couldn't read, trusting Glen as they did. *If they'd only known what a real creep he was…*

But what was there to know? Looking back on all of this, I feel like a real creep myself, for I was all too willing to blame my uncle for my desires and, what's worse, understand them as the product of a sexual abuse that never occurred. Then I consider that what's *truly creepy* is the extent to which my surrounding culture — everything in it from church to school to family to peers — had made such a perverse interpretation of my feelings not just a likely story but one I (and others) bent over backwards to concoct, despite all real evidence to the contrary. It's appalling. And as I write this, I'm scratching an itch on my arm until it bleeds. I have never been a cutter, but this little act of self-harm is my empathy for those who do cut. I'm punishing myself for the awfulness inflicted on me, for the awfulness I in turn thought of others, like my uncle. I'm revealing the scar deep down.

If Freud is right and the uncanny is in part about the repetition of the repressed, then my uncle figures as the return of that which much of the culture in south Louisiana during my childhood attempted to repress — not him per se but everything he stood for: the possibility of a queer life, somewhat sustainable, even pleasurable at times, striving to be free from bigotry, hatred, and abuse. But more radically, my uncle is creepy, not because he represents the return of a repressed fear of castration, but because he suggests the fundamental instability of the primacy of the family unit. He offered the possibility of an alternative genealogy — and that's what had to be repressed. I needed to get married, I needed my homoerotic desires to be explained away, I needed to follow the straight and narrow path. And I tried for a while, though my wife, goddess bless her, was, if not gay like me, at least queer enough that she needed to follow her own different path. I thank the universe we decided against children and that, when the time was right, we split amicably.

So, since Glen died and some imaginative possibilities were cut off for me, the genealogy had to go in another direction. While part of me may have been piecing together a story that made him the villain, another part of me knew that other narratives of queerness were out there. I'd at least seen enough of his life to sense this. And I knew, studying literature as I did in college and graduate school, that books contained those narratives. Indeed, I took from Uncle Glen an interest in the aesthetic. As opposed to my father, who wanted me to put down that copy of *Prince Caspian*, Glen encouraged my love of reading. For one birthday, me just on the cusp of adolescence, he gave me both a bookcase and a subscription to *National Geographic*. I remember my jaw literally dropping when he and his lover brought in he bookcase. He knew me. He recognized the budding nerd in me. And with the gift of the magazine, I think he recognized that I too would one day have to leave, need to journey out, go explore other ways of being, and I think the *NatGeos* were his way of telling me it would be okay, there would be amazing and wonderful places to discover.

Of course, I turned to the arts in the years after his death. It was a way to reject my father for rejecting me. Books, classical music, silly attempts at various art projects, then the piano and composing music. My mother had always wanted a piano, so, when finally financially secure enough to spend some money, my parents bought what we called a "wall unit," a solid instrument that could discreetly be used to display knick-knacks. A set of complimentary lessons came with the purchase, and my mother, who had learned a little piano as a child, started taking them. She was just too busy, though, to keep up with them, so she asked the teacher if I could take them over; I'd already started teaching myself from the music books she brought home. I'm not bragging when I say that I took to the instrument right away, and within two years was learning how to play the famous Rachmaninoff C# minor prelude.

Dumm... Dummm... DUMMMMMM....

The ominous octaves attracted me like no other sounds at the time, and I know I drove my parents a bit bonkers by practicing this piece so often. The teacher saw some talent and insisted that I continue the lessons, giving my parents a ridiculous discount for teaching me. When I could I'd save up money from babysitting and pay for my own lessons. I'd bike over interstate overpasses to get to the music studio. I loved the instrument, and still do. I immediately started writing music, page after page of penciled scribbles. I started to play in church, at first abominably and only persevered through the patience of some good Baptist folks who encouraged me. I wanted to be a musician, much to my parents' chagrin. I remember my mother telling me, on multiple occasions, that music was a great hobby, but not a career. *This isn't work.* But I played increasingly for money, first as a church musician, then accompanying singers at weddings. I made good pocket cash throughout my 20s. Still, I never seriously pursued music as a career. Part of me must have believed my parents deep down, but I never let music far out of my life. I play with friends to this day. And I count such music-making part of my legacy from my uncle.

At the time, though, my creepy uncle's legacy of the arts had to compete with other pressures to channel any innate aesthetic penchant I had into other, more legitimate forms of expression. And while one might be un-homed within your home, that home and its surrounding supporting communities are often invested in keeping you still contained within it. Classical music, an inheritance as it were from my uncle, allowed me to differentiate myself from others, especially my neglectful father, my vicious schoolmates. But church music, especially the hymns of the Baptist hymnal, shaped my sense of self in subtler and lasting ways. As a Baptist in the largely Catholic culture of New Orleans, attending Catholic schools, I encountered yet another differentiating layer between myself and others, but the hymns we sang on Sundays helped provide solace throughout the week. I'd whisper their propaganda to myself, turning my eyes upon Jesus, looking full in his wonderful face, while kids shouted faggot in my own.

Such hymns provided more than just mantras to survive the day. The Baptist hymnal taught me about poetry and love. We started going to our neighbor's Baptist church after my youngest sister was born. Dad had been present for her birth and was so moved by the experience that he insisted we find a church. Mother had been Catholic, but that was out, the Church having denied my mother the sacraments when she married my churchless father. So, we asked chain-smoking elderly Ms. Margie where she went to church, and Highland Baptist became a part of my life, in some ways one of the central parts of it, for the next decade.

I was 11, 12. Just entering puberty. I was ripe for understanding everything happening to me and my body — and the strange desires and fixations creeping up on me — through the language of the hymnal, those sweet and twisted poems that saw desire as only rightly directed toward our lord and savior. Indeed, if you have any experience of protestant hymnody, you know that the language of hymns is often intimate, even borderline erotic, full of discourses drawn from lovers' words.

Turn your eyes upon Jesus,
Look full in His wonderful face,
And the things of earth will grow strangely dim,
In the light of His glory and grace.[15]

Such words catch me by surprise even nearly forty years after I first heard them. As I write this, I'm sitting in a Japanese coffee shop in Irvine, California, and the tinkling piano music playing in the background is largely ambient, but a couple of strains penetrate into consciousness. I hear the tune of this old hymn, "Turn Your Eyes Upon Jesus," and I'm caught anew, snagged on sounds that I haven't heard in decades but that I recognize as part of my soul, having sucked them in so long ago. It's not unusual at all to hear hymns in such places; many Asian-American communities here are quite religious.

But what's perhaps a little more unusual is how the language of these hymns spoke simultaneously to someone like me about how Christ could help me overcome my sinful queer urges by, in some ways, becoming the object of them. One of my favorite hymns was "In the Garden," a homoerotic love song that I would frequently request at church.

I come to the garden alone,
While the dew is still on the roses,
And the voice I hear falling on my ear,
The Son of God discloses…

And He walks with me, and He talks with me,
And He tells me I am His own,
And the joy we share as we tarry there,
None other has ever known!

15 According to Wikipedia, the hymn "Turn Your Eyes Upon Jesus," whose chorus I can recite (and sing) in toto to this day, was written by Helen Howard Lemmel and first published in 1918. It's a standard in many hymnals, and I saw many copies in hymnals throughout my youth and young adulthood. You can find numerous versions readily available online.

He speaks and the sound of His voice,
Is so sweet the birds hush their singing,
And the melody that he gave to me,
Within my heart is ringing...[16]

I look back on this, hearing its strains in my ear, and can't help but think if there's anything gayer. All my adolescent queer body wanted to do was to "tarry," whatever the fuck that meant. But the hymns also poisoned as they taught about love; after all, what earthly love, especially something as debased as homosexuality, could compare to the soul-transporting bliss of Christ, whose chaste love could provide a joy "none other has ever known"?

More devastatingly, some of the hymns seemed to whisper the potential of death to make everything better. As a young man, a teenager, speaking softly to myself throughout the day the words to "Turn Your Eyes Upon Jesus," I couldn't help but hear a potential solution to my cursed state.

O soul, are you weary and troubled?
No light in the darkness you see?
There's light for a look at the Savior,
And life more abundant and free.

Through death into life everlasting
He passed, and we follow Him there;
O'er us sin no more hath dominion
For more than conqu'rors we are!

16 This classic hymn was written in 1912 by C. Austin Miles. Again, numerous versions are readily available online. It's been covered by many famous folks, and was sung religiously (pun intended) throughout my childhood, teenage, and young adult church-going days in the South.

His Word shall not fail you, He promised;
Believe Him and all will be well;
Then go to a world that is dying,
His perfect salvation to tell!

I so wanted to be a "conqu'ror"—what teen boy at the time wouldn't? Overcoming oneself while being saved from the fires of eternal damnation, or at least the burning of fleshly desire—such a potent poetry seemed designed specifically for me to hear.

And so, I learned to apologize for my creepiness very early on. I accepted Jesus Christ as my Lord and Savior during one Southern Baptist revival, and then we headed to Biloxi for vacation. All along the hour and a half journey I vowed to myself to keep my soul clean, but as we pulled into the Holiday Inn I was already frustrated with my sister, sinning in my heart. I knew I was fucked. I probably still have the little book that the preacher used to tutor my unsaved soul: I remember the pictures of the lost, little cartoon figures, headed over the bridge into hell. Perhaps I should've sped the journey, I used to think.

I didn't realize at the time the extent to which these voices, sung in collective unison and harmony every Sunday throughout my adolescence, were crafting my strongest sense of how I understood myself. But when I look back on the feeble attempts at poetry I tried at the time, I can see how these verses modeled both my own poetry making and my sense of the world.

I see a would-be lover
Passing by my side
And wonder where the joy would be
In letting passion ride.

I see the handsome face
Returns my deep desire;
I want to reach and touch and stroke
And satisfy the fire

Instead I turn my face
And look the other way
And wonder why I keep on going
When I would rather stay.

I see the would-be lovers
Passing by my side
And wonder where the joy could be
In making passion hide.

The imitation of form is apparent enough; the uptake of self-mortification and the longing to turn away from bodily desire more devastating. What I recall most about writing such poetry is doing it so alone, late at night, after everyone in the house had gone to bed. I'm 17, 18, staying up late to stare out the window while counting iambs, groping for rhymes, confessing my need to confess, even fetishizing my loneliness and pain before heading to bed to rub off some spunk into my briefs.

"Desire"

In bed I lay awake at night,
Obsessed with my obscene desire,
And try to find a way to drown
A soul that burns as though on fire.

And through the day the fight goes on
As I am tempted all the time;
Yet still I fight the fire that flames
And hide the secret that is mine.

I must admit that, even now, I like the alliteration here: the "fs" a fumbling toward understanding — and repressing — my own creeping desires. Indeed, repression is everywhere in these poems:

"Carnality"

The sin of my carnality
Is stabbing like a knife,
And my own hand controls the blade
Which brings upon my strife.

If only I would yield to God
And let Him reign within
I know the blade would go away
And peace would then begin.

To say the words and to have faith
Are very different though;
It's one thing to say, "God, come in!" –
Another to let go.

And yet until that time that I
Surrender to His rule,
My blade will keep on stabbing me
While I control the tool.

Control the tool, indeed. What a phallic metaphor that, at the time, I'm sure I had no consciousness of.

Unsurprisingly, perhaps, I became a huge fan of the work of Christina Rossetti, the Victorian poet par excellence of self-abnegation and self-denial, who wrote hundreds of verses about love denied while turning her own eyes to Jesus, or at least to a better life beyond death, or perhaps just to the cessation of desire in death.

Somewhere or other there must surely be
The face not seen, the voice not heard,
The heart that not yet — never yet — ah me!
Made answer to my word.

Somewhere or other, may be near or far;
Past land and sea, clean out of sight;
Beyond the wandering moon, beyond the star
That tracks her night by night.

Somewhere or other, may be far or near;
With just a wall, a hedge, between;
With just the last leaves of the dying year
Fallen on a turf grown green.[17]

I read this old poem now and think how resonant it is with the singer in Radiohead's "Creep," Rossetti's speaker herself on the verge of wondering if she, too, really belongs here. I turned such verses into music, composing little art songs that my adult friend Larry would sing in his rich baritone, voicing all the longing — of desire and my want to be released from it — that I couldn't articulate in my own words. I used art to theorize my desire.

But I was also steadily composing some other verse — and there is a lot of it, fumbling poetry that I've carted around for decades — that speaks to slightly other desires and needs, a wanting to acknowledge something taken from me, something denied.

---

17 While many (if not most) of Rossetti's poems are readily available online, the standard edition, one I owned as a young man, is the following: R.W. Crump (ed.), *The Complete Poems of Christina Rossetti* (Baton Rouge: Louisiana State University Press, 1979). I actually met Professor Crump, a serious scholar and lovely woman, just briefly while I was at LSU in the 1980s. She was even kind enough to write a short, glowing comment about an article I published about Rossetti's work and the sacred sensuality of its metaphors.

"A Need"

There are children
Who cannot say "Good-bye"
For they have no place
From which to leave
And farewells need a place.

There are children
Who cannot say "Hello"
For they have no place
At which to arrive
And greetings always need a place.

There are children
Who can only sit in silence
Saying nothing
For they have no place
To go or leave
And never learned the words
Of need and place.

I'd forgotten about this poem until I found it recently, buried in a box, and I have no recollection of the particular circumstances of composing it. But I must have been 20 or so, just beginning to recognize that I could occupy a different standpoint in relation to myself and the abuse I'd suffered, even if I had to externalize that standpoint and articulate it through a nameless, abstract "child." At the same time, the poem speaks to me from across nearly decades about something I knew deep in my heart, something about my own creepiness: I loved the people — at church, in my family, in my neighborhood — who, if they only knew me, the real me deep down, would've wanted nothing more to do with me.

What are the persistent voices, the ones that linger, that even now I can hear when I sit silently, or, having just woken up, don't feel quite defended against yet, the armor of daily tasks and preoccupations smothering the sounds of the past, muting the whispers that continue to tell the tale of my utter strangeness, my need to be outcast, thrown aside, at best neglected if not in fact forsaken? I often go through my day having imaginary conversations, processing in my mind various attacks and parries. I'm constantly hearing the voices of others criticizing, mocking, demanding justifications, and I rehearse responses, defenses, and counter-thrusts — mostly for exchanges that will never take place. I have to defend my desires, even just to myself, and feel puffed up with a kind of righteous indignation, a sense that I too prick when I bleed and deserve to be recognized as fully human. At other times, though, I'm so overwhelmed with remembered pain that my throat starts to close, as though my body has finally recognized the futility of living, of finding any sustaining happiness or contentment in a world that has already passed judgment, that won't acknowledge the legitimacy of my want, my need, my humanity.

Trying to open my throat to articulate the raw fact of my being in the world, however much it might not want me to be in it, prompted me to turn to narrative, storytelling, writing of all kinds in search of the words that I could use to shape my sense of self. Judith Butler reminds us in *Giving an Account of Oneself* that we are born into languages that predate us, that are already wildly circulating with meanings and meaningfulness. We can at best use this language given us, trying to take from it what we need.[18] These given words are the ones we try to make our own.

So, from early on, besides learning about music, I read a ton and figured that, if I wasn't going to be a musician, I could be an English teacher. So, I majored in English, and began to profes-

18 Judith Butler, *Giving an Account of Oneself* (New York: Fordham University Press, 2005).

sionalize my once furtive reading habits. And it was in reading that I learned more about queerness than nearly anywhere else. Music only got me so far. I remember once listening, perhaps at 15 or 16, to Tchaikovsky's Sixth Symphony, reading the liner notes and learning that part of the pathos of the work (it's called the "Pathetique") may very well have stemmed from the composer's homosexuality and an unfortunate love affair. I was shocked, even somewhat appalled, but also partly taken with the idea that music could express, if not articulate, such dilemmas. Writing, though, could speak to them even more directly and explicitly, and I sought out books that grappled with sexual difference.

I can't recall all the things I read, and it would be tedious for you, as a reader, to wade through such an accounting. But I learned from Walt Whitman how a writer could reach out and touch someone across great distances to talk about

> *Hours continuing long, sore and heavy-hearted [...].*
> *Hours when I am forgotten, (O weeks and months passing, but I believe I am never to forget!)*
> *Sullen and suffering hours! (I am ashamed — but it is useless — I am what I am;)*
> *Hours of my torment — I wonder if other men ever have the like, out of the like feelings*
> *Is there even one other like me — distracted — his friend, his lover, lost to him?).*[19]

How I thrilled to this poem, this cry of anguish, and the blasphemy of self-declaration — "I am what I am" — the very words god uses to describe himself. How dare the queer poet use the

19 Again, as with Rossetti, so many versions of Whitman's work are readily available online. I first found "Hours continuing long..." from a second-hand bookstore copy: *Whitman: Selections from Leaves of Grass* (The Laurel Poetry Series), edited by Richard Wilbur and introduced by Leslie A. Fiedler. My battered little copy was a second printing from 1960, which I still have to this day.

divine formula to justify his sin, to place it at the core of his being. Isn't this loneliness proof of his error, the fundamental flaw in being a faggot? Such verse spoke to me about my condition but also seemed to confirm simultaneously both its necessary abjection and its defiant stance. My own sense of pain and loss was turning, at times, to anger.

I took an independent study on the works of D.H. Lawrence. I'd wanted to study Evelyn Waugh since the television adaptation of *Brideshead Revisited* had made a huge impact on me when I saw it at 16 years of age, broadcast on PBS. Charles and Sebastian's youthful love affair seemed idyllic, even troubled as it was by family intrigue and alcoholism. Here were two boys clearly having a romance. And the scene of them getting caught sunbathing, Sebastian's sister smiling knowingly when stumbling upon them, has stayed with me for decades; Anthony Andrews and Jeremy Irons's young naked dimpled butts burned in my brain. No faculty member wanted to read Waugh with me, but one consented to Lawrence. And while I didn't love the work, I remember my absolute interest in the lesbian drama late in *The Rainbow* as well as the famous wrestling scene in its sequel, *Women in Love*. I sought out the Ken Russell film (with screenplay by Larry Kramer, which meant nothing to me at the time but could've been a signpost toward a different kind of life) and played several times the tape of Alan Bates and Oliver Reed grappling with one another in front of that fireplace.[20] I too wanted a friend I could undress with, touch, get close to like that. But I also felt like a creep watching this again and again, doing something furtive, hiding the tape, not wanting others to know what I was doing. I felt similar thrilling creepiness reading William Maxwell's largely forgotten classic *The Folded Leaf*, about two boys rooming together in school, one clearly having a crush on the other. There's a deliciously painful scene of the two sharing a bed in the depth of winter, sleeping back to back, the

20 If you haven't seen this film, you should: Ken Russell (dir.), *Women in Love*, Brandywine Productions/United Artists, 1969.

crushing boy sliding his foot across the bed to rest it against the foot of the other boy as he falls asleep. How I longed for a friend whose foot I could use to send me into peaceful slumber.

Such furtive reading only increased, and I remember the intense interest I had when Merchant Ivory filmed E.M. Forester's posthumously published *Maurice*. Faith, my older female friend, was remarkably patient about all of my interests in alternative sexualities, and while our church friends, Larry and Jeanie, wouldn't go see the film with us, Faith and I went to see it by ourselves, even buying and reading the book together. She must have known of my incipient queerness. What twenty-year-old straight kid is that interested in art films about faggots? She didn't make me feel creepy about my interest, though, and for that I remain grateful to this day, well over half a life away.

Lucky for me that the queer is a figure I could find readily enough in a lot of literature, even if that figuration often focused on the queer as lurking creep. Moving on from *The Chronicles of Narnia* and *The Lord of the Rings*, I turned from fantasy to science fiction and remember encountering the perverse Baron Harkonen in Frank Herbert's *Dune*, which I read at 15 or 16, and the David Lynch film adaptation which had just come out. Although a monster who, in the book, drugs his boys to keep them from resisting his advances, and who, in the film, fondles them before killing them, he was one of the few representations of powerful queerness I could find. Part of me was horrified. Another part of me fucking loved it. I felt myself the creepy Baron, the big fat man dripping with open sores, preying on the innocent. Ok, even if I wasn't the Baron (I was as thin as a rail), I feared that he was my future self, the monstrous predator that I could become. But at the same time, I relished the power he had. If he couldn't find others to share his fantasies, he could force them to comply. Indeed, the complexities and perverse attractions of the creepy queer are abundant in literature, and I sought them out, if not as models for myself, then perhaps as both cautionary tales and sources of furtive power.

Oscar Wilde's *The Picture of Dorian Gray* was a particular favorite.[21] I loved all of Wilde's work and tried to write about him, often badly, being too much of a fanboy. Dorian Gray, like Wilde's life itself, seemed to offer a powerful moral lesson: herein lies the path of debasement, doom, and destruction, self and otherwise. You wouldn't just destroy yourself, but you'd take others with you, wife, children, friends. Basil Hallward, the character who'd painted the infamous portrait that bears the record of Dorian's sins, his experiments in living solely for pleasure, confronts Dorian and asks, "Why is your friendship so fatal to young men?" We don't know much about how or why it is so fatal, but I could read into that question all of the perversities my heart feared and desired. Dorian was more than a creep. He was dangerous, and part of the danger was generated out of the homoeroticism that surrounded him, and that clung to the book itself as the product of a gay man sent to prison and dying in exile and disgrace for being queer. But Wilde had dared to present Dorian as an attractive and compelling figure, even if he's ultimately one whose charms and power lured other people to their doom. What joys they may have experienced beforehand, though — those I wanted to know.

But Dorian is also a creep, and the word appears sprinkled throughout *The Picture of Dorian Gray*, if not directly as an identifier for the ageless one himself but as a way for Wilde to cultivate a foreshadowing sense of doom and evil, with creeping mists and shadows, the paint of the portrait itself at times seeming to creep slowly into the demonic. Since discovering Baron Harkonen and Dorian I've long been fascinated by literary creeps, such as Patricia Highsmith's murderous Tom Ripley, who, unlike the various movie versions of him, is actually a successful and self-satisfied killer, taking his revenge on those who

21 I have so many versions of this book and of Wilde's works in general. I used the Project Gutenberg version for quotations and for my search for the word "creep," "The Picture of Dorian Gray by Oscar Wilde," http://www.gutenberg.org/files/174/174-h/174-h.htm.

have crossed him, especially on the noxious Dickie Greenleaf, who couldn't love him enough. And then there's Dennis Cooper, who has made a literary career of writing about gay serial killers in works like *Frisk*, older men preying on younger, wanting to open their bodies to see what's on the inside, but also all the more to possess and control them — perhaps ultimately punishing those who elicit in them strong feelings, desires, and attractions that can never fully be satisfied in the real world.[22] I feel just creepy admitting that I've enjoyed all of this work. And to be sure, Cooper's novels are complex fantasies, and I don't imagine he, as author, actually wants to enact what he describes. With that said, I know I have been drawn to them because, at moments, I have fantasized myself, if not killing an object of affection, at least turning my self-punishing impulses outward. Dear Matt, my undergrad film committee crush, suffered much in my tortured brain. I may not have been able to attract his attention in this world, but in the feverish rooms of my brain I jerked off many a night to images of tying him to my bed, face down, shaving his ass, and then sodomizing him with various glass bottles and stiff fruits. I would have left no permanent damage. I'm not a psychopath. But I won't lie: my late adolescent cock hardened into sadistic resolve. His body needed to feel my humiliation.

I feel I am hardly alone with such fantasies. The larger literary culture, at least, seems bent on making something of a fetish of experiences of suffering, with recent novels seeming to delight in their characters being put through their torturous paces. Hanya Yanagihara's 2015 novel, *A Little Life*, is certainly a book that asks us to hold our gaze on creepiness.[23] A controversial and

---

22 Frank Herbert's *Dune*, Patricia Highsmith's *The Talented Mr. Ripley*, and Dennis Cooper's *Frisk* have all been made into films, as partially suggested above, and each book and film is worth seeking out to read and watch. The film version of *Frisk* may be the most challenging to find, and it's not terribly good, though I might call it goodly terrible.

23 I don't quote from this book, but feel compelled nonetheless to cite it, as it's worth seeking out and reading, despite its substantial girth: Hanya Yanagihara, *A Little Life: A Novel* (New York: Doubleday, 2015).

widely discussed novel, the mammoth book is perhaps most notable for its extended scenes—amounting to hundreds of pages—of tortured recounting of a young man, Jude, variously abused by his foster caretakers, including brothers in a religious order, a sadistic doctor, and a narcissistic boyfriend. Ostensibly about the communities of friendship that emerge to care for one another in the face of such damage, *A Little Life* has a hard time turning away from depictions of utter human cruelty, implicating readers in the voyeuristic act of looking at suffering born out of depravity. The length of the book becomes extravagant in its melodramatic and gothic rendering of its primary character's suffering as well as the incredible creepiness of those who inflict it. As critic Daniel Mendelsohn put it,

> But the wounds inflicted on Jude by the pedophile priests in the orphanage where he grew up, by the truckers and drifters to whom he is pimped out by the priest he runs away with, by the counselors and the young inmates at the youth facility where he ends up after the wicked priest is apprehended, by the evil doctor in whose torture chamber he ends up after escaping from the unhappy youth facility, are nothing compared to those inflicted by Yanagihara herself.[24]

Mendelsohn even refers to the experience of reading the novel as watching a striptease, witnessing a creepily exploitative disrobing of someone's tortured life. And yet, for all of the finely detailed rendering of pain and the attention to the interior struggles of its characters, *A Little Life* spends next to no energy, even in 800 pages, considering the socio-cultural structures or values that enable, allow, or perhaps even condone such suffering. The Catholic Church, educational systems, welfare organizations— we're led to believe that such institutions just serve as vectors of cruelty, and we are never told why.

---

24 Daniel Mendelsohn, "A Striptease Among Pals," *The New York Review of Books,* December 3, 2015, http://www.nybooks.com/articles/2015/12/03/striptease-among-pals/.

The bare existence of cruelty is, in its own way, haunting, perhaps even undeniable. People are cruel. But I want someone to blame, some accounting that explains how I was preyed upon, perhaps as a way to understanding my own cruelty, my own creepiness. Yanagihara's is one way to approach intense creepiness, implicating the reader in his or her own creepy gaze. Reading the novel is akin to looking at that Diesel ad of a young man pressing down on the head of an older man about to lick his shoe. Such work reminds us of the creepiness in all of us, but I want something more. Acknowledgment of a pervasive interior predisposition or possibility doesn't seem sufficient, a bit to reifying of a Freudian trope into a universal truth. It's a start, but what might a prolonged gaze on creepiness allow us to see? Can we connect the dots between creepiness deeply felt and the contours of a life taking shape in a particular place or time, in a particular body?

&

J.R. Ackerley (1896–1967) was well aware of the damage wrought by homophobia, but instead of lamenting his queer fate in a homophobic world, he seemed instead hell-bent on delighting in his perversity, even his creepiness. He was a good-looking man and successful editor, who for twenty-four years worked as literary editor of the BBC's *The Listener*. He was friends with many of the major writers of his day, including E.M. Forester, and he published four books that, since his death, have only grown in popularity, all four recently reissued as part of the New York Review Book series. He was also something of a creep.

Literary scholar Piers Gray calls Ackerley one of his "marginal men," along with Ivor Gurney and Edward Thomas, men who stand in the relationship of "stranger" to the larger culture, allowing them some purchase as insider outsiders to comment on it. In Ackerley's case, homosexuality provided the basis for his estranging marginality—a marginality that Ackerley bravely, for the time, explored in his often exquisite prose. As Gray puts it, "His anarchic revisions of existence freed the imagination, let it at liberty to ponder our varied enslavements. His art was obsessed by this irony. He thus was ensnared by his illusions of freedom; the tragic desire to let language tell it all. What else is it there for? What other purpose can it or we have?"[25]

And telling it all seems to be at the heart of Ackerley's project. His posthumously published memoir, *My Father and Myself* (1968) is one of the earliest and most important full-length books in the 20th century to speak frankly, openly, and relatively unapologetically about homosexuality. Sex outside the norm marks the book from its opening sentence, which famously declares, "I was born in 1896 and my parents were married in 1919."[26] We are immediately put in the land of sexual impropriety. Something is queer here, with more to come, rest assured.

In elegant prose, Ackerley carefully describes his relationship with his father, a complex businessman, who, we discover, is head of two different families — something Ackerley and his siblings don't really discover until after his death. Ackerley's achievement here lies in offering an often moving account of a relationship that is simultaneously distant and loving, one not characterized by any kind of recognizable intimacy but nonetheless oddly accepting, father and son tolerant of one another's foibles. In one passage, the author describes his father attempting to talk about sex to the young Ackerley, who would sometimes bring home boys he fancied; his father, seizing a moment,

> took occasion to add — getting it all off his chest in one and providing for the future as well as the present — that in the matter of sex there was nothing he had not done, no experience he had not tasted, no scrape he had not got into and

---

25 Piers Gray, *Marginal Men: Edward Thomas, Ivor Gurney, J. R. Ackerley* (London: Macmillan, 1991), 115–16.

26 J.R. Ackerley, *My Father and Myself* (New York: New York Review Books, 1999), 7. Kudos to the *New York Review Books* line of attractive reprints that has reissued Ackerley's books, including *Hindoo Holiday.*

> out of, so that if we should ever be in want of help or advice we need never be ashamed to come to him and could always count on his understanding and sympathy.[27]

Ackerley confesses to not appreciating the import of the speech at the time, but it becomes increasingly clear to readers that Ackerley's interest in describing his father's sexual exploits, as fascinating as they are in their own right, is at least as equally invested in creating an opportunity for discussing his own. Perhaps Ackerley wagers that, in light of his father's shenanigans, a mid-century reader will be less likely to cast aspersions on his own.

And there's a lot to discuss. Ackerley is quite the slut, from his school days on. He offers lots of throwaway comments about his extra-curricular exploits, at one point describing himself as "predatory" on the prowl for boys to fuck.[28] The predation continues into his adulthood, with a lot of sex found through standing drinks or covering costs for needy young men. Ackerley slyly tells us that, "[t]hough I can't remember my state of mind at this period, I expect that much of all this seemed fun. It certainly afforded pleasure and amusement, it was physically exciting, and in England it had the additional thrill of risk."

On one hand, the bravery of persisting in sexual "deviancy" given the criminalization of homosexuality at the time seems almost admirable, committed as it is to the pursuit of pleasure at a time when such could result in real jail time:

> Industrious predator though I was, I was not a bold or reckless one. One of my father's yarns concerned a man who told a friend that whenever he saw an attractive girl he went straight up to her and said, "Do you fuck?" "My word!" said the friend. "Don't you get an awful lot of rebuffs?" "Of

27 Ibid., 107.
28 Ibid., 161.

> course," was the reply; "but I also get an awful lot of fucking." I was not in the least like that. I did not want rebuffs or cuffs, nor did I want the police summoned.[29]

On the other hand, descriptions of such risky pursuits are often laced with a peculiar poignance, for, above all else, what Ackerley spent his life looking for was an "Ideal Friend":

> The Ideal Friend was always somewhere else and might have been found if only I had turned a different way. The buses that passed my own bus seemed always to contain those charming boys who were absent from mine; the ascending escalators in the tubes fiendishly carried them past me as I sank helplessly into hell. Unless I had some actual business or social engagement (often maddening, for then, when punctuality or responsibility was unavoidable and I was walking with my host or guest, the Ideal Friend would be sure to appear and look deep into my eyes as he passed) I seldom reached my destination, but was forever darting off my buses, occupied always, it seemed, by women or Old Age Pensioners, because on the pavements below, which I was constantly scanning, some attractive boy had been observed.[30]

This search for the ideal friend is one with which nearly any reader could potentially sympathize, and it only assumes a creepier cast when Ackerley gets specific about what precisely he's looking for:

> What I meant by the Ideal Friend I doubt if I ever formulated, but now, looking back over the years, I think I can put him together in a partly negative way by listing some of his many disqualifications. He should not be effeminate, indeed preferably normal; I did not exclude education but did not want it, I could supply all that myself and in the loved one

29 Ibid., 172.
30 Ibid., 171–72.

> it had always seemed to get in the way; he should admit me but no one else; he should be physically attractive to me and younger than myself—the younger the better, as closer to innocence; finally he should be on the small side, lusty, circumcised, physically healthy and clean: no phimosis, halitosis, bromidrosis. It may be thought that I had set myself a task so difficult of accomplishment as almost to put success purposely beyond my reach; it may be thought too that the reason why this search was taking me out of my own class into the working class, yet still toward that innocence which in my class I had been unable to touch, was that guilt in sex obliged me to work it off on my social inferiors. …if asked then I would probably have said that working-class boys were more unreserved and understanding, and that friendship with them opened up interesting areas of life, hitherto unknown.[31]

I quote from this book at length because, in many ways, such a description is hardly out of step with a certain kind of mid-twentieth-century English homosexual bourgeois sensibility that's not without historical interest, especially since it contains elements of a personal ad that actually persists into contemporary gay circles. In terms of the former, the penchant of upper middle-class English men for working class toughs is well documented; the allure of male coupling was fueled as much by class transgression as the forbidden fruit of the homoerotic. Ackerley's patronage of young, struggling men is a common enough trope for the time, an outright stereotype, but also one that gestures to a larger gay male subcultural formation that anachronistically styles itself on ancient Greek pederasty: the intergenerational male couple, an older man supporting a younger lover on whom he dotes. While perhaps a bit less common in the twenty-first century than before, with young people needing less and less an entrée into gay (secret, hidden) subcultures,

31 Ibid., 163–64.

other elements of Ackerley's wish list still ring true: no fats, no femmes, for instance.

Ackerley's creepiness comes full-force when he transmogrifies his real-life search for the ideal friend through the fantasies of fiction. His one published novel, *We Think the World of You*, is a thinly veiled autobiographical account of one such failed relationship with a potential ideal friend. The narrator recounts his courting of a down-and-out working class youth, with whom he has developed a periodic sexual relationship, but also, curiously, a relationship with the boy's family, a mother and father in particular. In a more strained way, he also knows the boy's girlfriend as well, who seems to put up with the older man (as do the parents) because he is so often ready to pick up the tab and to provide other forms of financial support. The title reflects the catch phrase that the family keeps telling him to thank him for his generosity—"we think the world of you"—but it often rings false in his ears. Indeed, perhaps because he is generous with them, and they in turn seem so stinting in appreciation, providing access to Johnny only in dribs and drabs, the narration describes constant feelings of being let down, ignored, or given the short end of the stick. He positively nags and he steadily becomes a pest, always demanding more time with Johnny, complaining when Johnny doesn't show up for a date because he is spending time with his parents or girlfriend. Things come to a head when he starts taking care of the family dog while Johnny does a short stint in jail. The narrator seems to switch his attentions from Johnny to the dog, whom the family doesn't want to relinquish. Consequently, the narratives turn to a series of strange and strained episodes, in which the dog becomes the focus of a tug-of-war between a family and a creepy old man, the animal standing in for the absent Johnny.

Ackerley's narrator comes to some self-consciousness of his own creepiness toward the end of the novel, recognizing the oddity of the situation he himself has instigated:

> I found myself afflicted by a despondency which had nothing to do with the perception that I had been put, to a large extent, in the wrong. Say what one might against these people, their foolish frames could not bear the weight of iniquity I had piled upon them; they were, in fact, perfectly ordinary people behaving in a perfectly ordinary way, and practically all the information they had given me about themselves and each other had been true, had been real, and not romance, or prevarication, or the senseless antics of some incomprehensible insect, which were the alternating lights in which, since it had not happened to suit me, I had preferred to regard it.[32]

These "ordinary" folks "behaving in a perfectly ordinary way" make Ackerley's narrator seem the creep he is, an interloper, someone who has thrust himself on them, trying in some way to be a part of their family, but in a sexual way (the son's sometime male lover) for which there were (and are) no "ordinary" ways to understand or accommodate. The creepiness of the situation lies precisely in the ways in which it transgresses normative family relations, while also *insisting* that the transgression be recognized as valuable, as something that should be perfectly acceptable. The narrator's recognition of the creepiness he has created here is accompanied by near despair: "Yes, it was true, and it had all been useless. I saw it now and how pitiful it was. It had been a mistake from beginning to end, the total struggle, all that love and labor, passion and despair; it had all been hopeless and unavailing; I had lost the fight for him before ever it had begun."[33] We almost start to feel sorry for him; he seems a potentially queer outsider, storming the gates of normativity, but even here he seems to nag us, his readers for a sympathy that might be too much to ask for.

32 J.R. Ackerley, *We Think the World of You* (New York: New York Review Books, 2000), 171.

33 Ibid., 192

For many, Ackerley's interest in intergenerational relationships itself might seem inherently creepy, but I totally understand it. While a young man, I sought out the company of older men, if not at the time to sleep with them, then certainly to replace the emotional neglect from my own father with other forms of male-male intimacy. My older friend Larry was really exemplary in this regard, providing companionship, advice, and support for my aesthetic interests. Since I didn't come out until I was well into my late 20s, I was already approaching the age (at least in gay circles) where *I* was the "older man" who would be looking for a younger lover. That aside, though, I'd *always* longed not just for an older male friend (which I'd found in Larry) but an "ideal friend," someone my own age with whom I could explore mutual desires. I had friends, surely, but never for too long. I was just too unstable, too cold and then too needy, and my closest friends were inevitably women, with whom I could share emotionally in ways that I couldn't with, or that weren't tolerated by, other young men.

As such, I carry with me to this day a strong sense of lack: I have no lasting male friendships from my youth. And while I have formed more sustaining attachments with men in my middle-age, I miss a sense of continuity, a shared history with men who have known me for more than a decade. Ackerley may have missed such as well. He rarely talks about long-term friendships. Instead he's always talking about his young men, and wanting to make those relationships (not always, but occasionally, with the right boy) last. I get that too, though perhaps in ways different than Ackerley may have. If you haven't had the close companionship of boys as a young man — and I didn't, my creepy, cross-eyed, non-athletic, slightly femmy self being so very off-putting for most boys — then you might try to recover it later. I can only speculate on Ackerley's behalf, projecting my own senses of loss and lack. But I can certainly identify the creepiness of it, the older man constantly courting the young, trying to befriend them.

Indeed, what draws me to Ackerley's writing and his search for the ideal friend is precisely what's creepy in it — the lifelong yearning that's just a little bit suspect because it lies outside the bounds of what's normal but is, in its own way, a version of it. Ackerley's desire for an ideal friend, particularly a younger friend, collapses the marriage and paternal bonds into one. He wanted a lover *and* a son, a dense intimacy that would offer adult companionship while also filling the void left by his own distant — because he had a whole other family — father. The collapsing seems creepy, or even in the Freudian sense "uncanny," because it mixes things that are normally separate — or perhaps it reveals the hidden erotics of such relations that we normally keep repressed. But however creepy it might be, I can totally understand it. My father's emotional neglect of me haunts me to this day, and my uncle's untimely death seems a lost opportunity to have experienced an alternative home in my youth. So, I have spent a lot of time trying to construct that home, to have that family, and, as I've aged, to be a father to the son that I didn't have myself. And at times that construction has bordered on the creepy.

Not quite like Ackerley's creepiness. For him, his dog Tulip, an Alsatian bitch, became the family he yearned for, even his ideal friend, a relationship he recounts at some length in his memoir of their friendship, *My Dog Tulip*. But even in *My Father and Myself*, Ackerley is often at his most lucid and poetic when writing about the dog: "Yet looking at her sometimes I used to think that the Ideal Friend, whom I no longer wanted, perhaps never had wanted, should have been an animal-man, the mind of my bitch, for instance, in the body of my sailor, the perfect human male body always at one's service through the devotion of a faithful and uncritical beast."[34] There are truly odd — and yes, creepy — moments of intense physical interaction between Ackerley and Tulip, particularly when the dog is in heat: "In truth, her love and beauty when I kissed her, as I often did, sometimes

34 Ibid., 282.

stirred me physically; but though I had to cope with her own sexual life [...] the thought of attempting to console her myself, even with my finger, never seriously entered my head."[35] But there's also poignant beauty in their friendship, something more fulfilling for Ackerley than he had ever found with people: "She offered me what I had never found in my sexual life, constant, single-hearted, incorruptible, uncritical devotion, which it is in the nature of dogs to offer. She placed herself entirely under my control. From the moment she established herself in my heart and home, my obsession with sex fell whole away from me."[36] Did it fall away, or was it channeled elsewhere? Or, to put that creepy question another way, did Ackerley want a perfect body, a perfect soul? And did he wonder, at times, even with the comfort of his dog at his side, what the hell he was doing here?

We *creeps* ask ourselves such questions all the time, but who perhaps *isn't* trying to find solace, a path through a livable life? We are all creeping up on our own answers to how we deal with the families into which we are born, the relations set in motion as we come into being, the languages used to nurture and abuse us into the lives we come to lead. Ackerley's relationship with his dog was one way of dealing with the creep within, of working out one's relations to find at least the semblance of contentment. Who am I to deride what he finds with Tulip? My own choices, which I recount in the next section of this book, my apologia, have tended not toward the animal world, though I have loved my pets, and have thought of them as much more than pets, but true animal companions, beings we are privileged to share time and space with, for whom we cultivate the capacity to care. Beyond such companions, though, I have searched for and at times cobbled together my own family of sorts, a found family, following the queer mantra that friends are the family you choose. And in such making there is often more than a bit of creepiness, as Adam Kotsko reminds us in *Creepiness*. I have probably been

35 Ibid., 281–82.
36 Ibid., 280–81.

Steve Urkel, the unwanted neighbor who nonetheless becomes a central member of a group that doesn't quite know what to do with him.

There is a young journalist and comics lover whom I hope will read these words and understand me better, and why our friendship was fraught at times. There's a young trumpet player and gaming geek whom I hope will better understand what it is I tried to do, what I was asking for. Walt Whitman, whom I read and wrote about at length in my own youth, says that he hopes to reach out and touch you through his words, whoever you are now holding his book in hand. I always thought that gesture, whenever I came across it in his poetry, just a little bit creepy, but also perhaps delightfully so. At this point in my life, that's the kind of creepiness I can live with, and I hope my comparable gestures to the young men I have loved, whom I thought of as potential "ideal friends," is less creepy than an attempt to foster understanding. Perhaps it can only ever be both in such cases.

These books and experiences have laid out paths for tracing and thinking about that creeping. Is such a theory of creepiness? Creepiness might remain too capacious a category to be fully theorizable, but therein might lie both its complexity and its usefulness. At the very least, I have remaining to me my apologia, my attempt to show how I have tried to put my own creepiness to use.

An Apology

"The boy looks up
As the grieving sound of his own begetting
Keeps on."
—Allen Grossman

I was identified early in life as s creep. Now I'm trying to figure out how to survive as one. Damage shapes the mind. My perceptions craft my paranoid experience of the world. But is such paranoia purely psychological? Is it not also in some ways justified, a survival mechanism? Further, can my creepiness be used strategically to reveal the structures and values that make some lives less livable? Put the question another way: how can I creep without being creepy?

My memoir and theorizing in the previous sections have been attempts to approach such questions, just as much as they have been attempts to recover what was lost, what was taken, from my youth. Like the minimalist music I loved as a teen, I rehearse the same themes and questions over and over, pounding the chord again and again and listening for the telling differences in the repeating arpeggios. I think a similar impulse has been at play in the recovery of the word "queer," another term with which I have a strong set of identifications. The emergence of the word queer as a rallying cry in the immediate throes of the AIDS epidemic and then in the scholarly halls of academe and the rise of queer theory have called attention to how many LGBTQ folk are not in fact damaged, sick, twisted perverts, but actually offer critical insights about the social, cultural, and political structures that actively position people along a spectrum of health (or disease) tied to their sexual behaviors and interests. Being queer is less a designation of an innate condition and more the potential to see the workings of power through bodies and lives. In so many ways, we come to our identifications not just to know ourselves but to find a place — from privileged to abject to resistant — in a social hierarchy.

But queerness is different than creepiness, and I don't think I want to mount a defense of creepiness in quite the same way that would recover it as a term of resistant identification. Queerness should be cultivated. I'm less sure about creepiness. There are some forms of creepiness of which we should be wary. But I do think we should push our comfort zones about what we find creepy. For we have pathologized some forms of creepiness that are really more about curiosity and the desire to make connections -attributes and proclivities worth cultivating. At the very least, I understand from even just having written this book that so much of my own creepiness was given to me — in part through my queerness and the lingering associations between creepiness and homosexuality, but also because of the intense homophobia with which I grew up, cultivating within me, feelings of fear and self-loathing that made me hide — made me *look* as though I had something to hide — that made me seem creepy.

Still, I sense the need to defend my creepiness, to offer something of an apologia, even if it's a thing, this creepiness, more given to me than cultivated. But wait: I know that's not entirely accurate. To this day, I carry within me that sense of creepiness that profoundly shapes my expression of desires. What do I like? I like the furtive thing, the somewhat covert expression of desire. The subtle glances. Catching an eye, turning away, wondering if I was found out. I get turned on by secrets. But I somehow want to be caught. There's a doubleness here.

The covert and coded fascinate me because of that doubleness — the need to hide but also the itch to reveal a secret. I remember changing for PE and the kid next to me, someone

I barely knew, started complaining about the school's uniform requirement. He seemed particularly upset that the coaches had dictated to us what kinds of underwear were and were not acceptable: briefs, not boxers, jockstraps even better. We were 15, maybe 16, and I kept looking aslant at him while we both quickly changed, skinny legs sticking out of the required white briefs. To this day, I'm somewhat aroused by this exchange. Was he trying to communicate something to me, talking about his underwear? A normal boy wouldn't think so, I'm sure. But since normal boys seemed to have no trouble communicating with one another, then surely those of us not normal needed some kind of cue to exchange information, register interests, to connect. I'll never know. But the sheer possibility, wrapped in the covert, excited me. Many young queers today can come out, can more readily identify one another, but that just wasn't true of those of us growing up in less enlightened areas just a few decades ago. In all of my educational experiences, through the completion of my PhD at 25 years of age, I never — never — met an openly gay teacher. Some were surely gay. I *know* now some were. But precisely the lack of disclosure, and the necessity of signaling either interest or identity in some other way, has indelibly marked the discursivity of my own desires, how I understand them, how I enact them, how they are to me. So, I have played out the fantasy of that boy in the changing room a million times, wondering if the man I'm talking to is trying to tell me something, if we could slip away somewhere secretly and do our thing, returning to the light of day different but not recognized, except to each other.

I enjoy the little things, that must remain little, that perhaps have more significance because they must remain so. I'm sitting in a Peet's early this morning, writing, but also scoping out the boys in their gym shorts, looking for a little caffeinated rush before hitting the gym. Do they suspect the little thrill they give me? At my age, surely, it's a *little* rush, more a tickling in my briefs, but I squirm in my upholstered booth nonetheless, massaging something that still seems alive, even vital after all these years. A *deep down* thing.

But the covert never remains just so. Take this boy I run across, for instance. Walking across campus, I nearly strut, feeling my power. I have become aware of how I stare people down, feeling the pleasure in eyes averted. A student I know tangentially, someone who has approached me without much success, seems weasely as he passes by me, afraid to gesture in recognition, his lowered eyes darting quickly left to right. Perhaps I won't see him if he doesn't make eye contact. Indeed, I learned early to be a predator, a nearly clichéd trajectory for one so often a victim. We become our experiences. But my predation is generally harmless, just a fleeting creepiness at the corners, or a creepy conversation that happens only in my own mind. At the very least, I've been damaged enough by others that not only am I covert, but I'm always watching them carefully, wondering when they might strike next—wondering how I might strike first.

Watching others is surely an activity that can border on creepiness, and it's one that's been particularly difficult for me as a cross-eyed person, and my crossed-eye has no doubt played a role in giving me a creepy look. An article in *Cosmopolitan*, "9 Things That Make a Dude a 'Creep,' According to Science," listed the following, amongst other indicators, of creepiness: "He watches you before interacting," "He touches you frequently," "He steers the conversation toward sex," "He likes to take pictures of you," "He has greasy hair," and "He never looks you in the eye."[1] Now I'm well aware that *Cosmo* is hardly the most vetted source of reliable information (despite the tag line of assurance: "According to Science"), but I have seen similar reports with nearly identical lists circulating on the Web for some months. And I cannot deny that my already confessed penchant for taking pictures of guys, however surreptitiously, makes me

1 Hayley MacMillen, "9 Things That Make a Dude a 'Creep,' According to Science," *Cosmopolitan*, November 3, 2016, http://www.cosmopolitan.com/sex-love/a8102041/creepy-men-behaviors-study/.

creepy, and would confirm my creepiness to those around me if they knew. For all I know, my creepiness *has* been so confirmed by some who may have spied me taking a picture of a dude. But my general unwillingness to look people in the eye stems from my desire *not to* have people notice that I'm cross-eyed. I'm still, to this day, ashamed of having what used to be called a "lazy eye." The obvious asymmetricality that it gives my face is one of the traditional markers of ugliness. While a beauty mark is acceptably asymmetrical, a crossed-eye is not, perhaps in large part because people wonder if you're actually looking at them — which, as we know from *Cosmo*, signals creepiness. So, I'm forever in a real double-bind if I want to reduce my overall creep effect.

And the pressure either to correct or compensate for the crossed-eye is high. After all, who can forget Jack Nicholson's frightening visage, eyes veering toward one another, as he peeks through the door in *The Shining*. This is the iconic image of insane horror, the creep gone psycho. But even before that film came out in 1980, my parents were on the case, hauling me to the ophthalmologist to see what could be done about my unsettling look. For some time as a child, I wore a patch over my stronger eye, in what would become an increasingly futile attempt to strengthen the muscles around the "lazy" eye. If my crossed-eye made other children a bit wary of me, the patch didn't help. In fact, if you've ever seen someone with a patch over an eye in public, you have probably been a bit unsettled. Such seems only natural, as I reflect on it; our sight is one of our most precious senses, so damage to it is disturbing. Surely a crossed eye seems like damage — a lessening of visual power, a reminder that not all of us see as well as others, and that we are all headed eventually to the great darkening, the final turning off of the lights.

As noted, I was made aware early of the weirdness of my (quite literal) view on the world by other children, my would-be playmates, our first real critics: they generally either shied away from me, shunning my freakish visage, or pointed out directly my botched condition. Eventually one young man just told me directly that the problem was that I didn't look people in the eye. And that, consequently, made me seem... weird. His honest assessment of the situation hit me like a revelation. So, I spent innumerable hours training myself to look more directly in the eyes of my interlocutors. But such a move can elicit some uncomfortable interactions, for both parties. Many folks, in the midst of conversation, move a bit to the left or right, trying to figure out, practically unconsciously it seems, if I'm still looking at them. When I call on students in class, acknowledging a raised hand, they often wonder if I am in fact calling on *them*, or perhaps the person next to them, or someone else entirely. This must be a disconcerting experience, and I have tried to laugh it off, especially when a student asks, confusedly, "Are you looking at me?" I quip: "I'm looking at *all* of you." Sometimes nervous laughter follows, sometimes not. Even someone who has since become one of my dearest friends, when we first sat down for lunch together, kept shifting in her seat, trying to determine which of my eyes was indeed looking at her. She's a blunt gal originally from Missouri, and she couldn't help but show me with her bodily gyrations of discomfort that I should show her better what I was really looking at.

Part of what must have contributed to my sense of shame, my desire to hide my crossed eye and turn –however creepily– away from others is the relative absence of others who are noticeably crossed-eyed. You just don't see many of these folks. And when you do, you tend not to forget the experience. I can remember every lazy-eyed person I've interacted with, no matter how insignificant the encounter. The overweight student who herself wouldn't quite look me in the eye, no matter how much I tried to catch her gaze in the profoundest empathy. The travel agent booking my flight to San Diego who daringly didn't hide behind glasses; she was approaching her senior years and probably realized that people just weren't looking at her anymore. The collaborator who keeps her pleasant face hidden behind an array of increasingly spectacular glasses and a wave of blond hair covering half her face, one eye included. The game designer and media scholar who affected such a badass attitude that you almost didn't notice his crossed eye because you were more attuned to the verbal barbs launched from his mouth. This is a litany of compensations, of strategies to draw attention away from the eyes, except perhaps in the case of the older woman, who may not have given a shit anymore. Of course, some people are just plain lucky and don't need to do much to avert the inquiringly confused gazes of those wondering at whom you're looking. A list of "40+ Celebrities with Wonky Eyes" lists, at the top: Paris Hilton, Ryan Gosling, and Heidi Klum as people whose eyes don't quite line up.[2] I couldn't stand to look further down the list because, as I gazed at these beautiful people, sure enough, their eyes were somewhat unaligned. But who gives a fuck? Their sheer attractiveness otherwise so overcompensates for any oddity of the eye. They may be creepy in other ways (I don't know, not knowing them or paying much attention to contemporary celebrities), but they won't be creepy because of their eyes.

But I remain a bit creepy and increasingly don't mind. In fact, I have leaned more recently toward the practice of looking at people directly and all but daring them to notice or remark upon my crossed-eye. Of course, this strategy results in its own intensification of creepiness. Remember *Cosmo*: "He watches you before interacting." A corollary of that signal is "He stares at you." A fine balance is at play here. If you don't look people in the eye, they think you're a creep; if you do so to excess, they think you're a creep. In a spirit of advocacy for all who are ashamed of their lazy eyes, I have opted for the latter creepiness. Such seems like a queer reclaiming, a challenge to normative standards of beauty. Consequently, though, not many people enjoy talking to me, I wager. I make no apology.

---

2 *Ranker*, n.d., http://www.ranker.com/list/celebrities-with-strabismus/celebrity-lists.

And I continue to look, to probe with my eyes, my mobile technology vectoring a bit of my creepy watching, as it probably does for a lot of folks. I have already admitted to surreptitiously taking quick snaps of guys' butts. Just on the subway today, coming back home from visiting a colleague in Hollywood, I'm standing next to a young guy, buff, cute in a rough trade way, muscle shirt, backwards baseball cap, khaki shorts that hug his tight ass. I stand behind him so he can't see me ogle him. I take out my phone, pretending to check messages, but who am I kidding: there's no connectivity underground. I snap ten, fifteen pictures of this guy's ass. It's almost like I can't help it. And then I'm reversing the camera to take pictures of myself. To be fair, I take more selfies throughout the day than anything else (obsessively checking the cleanliness of my nose), and I don't *frequently* take pictures of other people without them knowing. But I do, often enough. And I go back and forth, snapping pics of the cute and unsuspecting, more often than not just their asses, and then my own face: back and forth, ass and face. And then, at home before I leave for work, I'll snap a few of my own ass, sometimes in my briefs, sometimes my khaki-clad butt, checking myself out in the mirror, a late Lacanian mirror stage, and I wonder what I'm doing. *Am I real enough? Do I have a perfect body?*

What the hell am I doing here?

It's a complicated creepiness, fetishizing these pics of my own and strangers' asses, looking at them throughout the day, visual mantras that give me a little charge, that seem a bit dangerous to check out with others in the room, thinking I'm checking messages, responding to texts. I creepily queer my day this way, introducing a bit of the erotic, the auto-erotic into a departmental meeting, a lunch with a colleague, a walk from building to building.

Indeed, I confess, perhaps the creepiest thing I do is my covert snapping of pictures of guys. Standing in line or walking through a mall, it's all too easy to take out your phone, looking as though you are responding to a message or declining a call, when in fact you are taking a photo of a body part that has attracted your attention, snagged your gaze. I love the little bit of underpants peeking out of the top of low-riding shorts. I feel myself constantly on the hunt for such sightings. Yesterday I caught a bit of waistline, briefs or maybe boxer briefs, Champion brand. I passed by the young man sitting bent over his laptop, and then passed by again, catching another glimpse of his gray shorts. Champion — an inexpensive brand, perhaps a working boy, or not someone who cares much about the brand of underwear he buys and wears, probably not lingering over the packages like I do, imagining how such underwear will make me feel as I walk through the world in it.

I sound like a fetishist, and so I am. Underwear fascinates me. Ever since I was a kid and saw bits of it sticking out of guys' pants, I eagerly look for those signs of the hidden, those pieces that snuggle against the privates, the additional layering keeping us from one another, protecting. My trainer wears Under Armour, a fun brand that hugs the skin. He probably wears it because it wicks away sweat from his body, keeping him dry and clean. But the name alone — Under *Armour* — suggests a need to protect the goods inside, with an added gesturing toward suiting up to do battle. But I still hear the slipperiness of armour into amour, the phallic package and curving buttocks sheathed in clothes that safeguard them but also show them off, inviting touch, stroking, caressing, fondling.

Ok, I creep myself out because I imagine but never touch. Unless one counts the (admittedly invasive) covert photographing. Is that a form of touching? Maybe what's creepy is just my following and not following through and making the pass, asking for the fuck. My creepy behavior strikes me as insufficiently goal oriented. And maybe that's the problem. I walk around admiring men's behinds, even collecting images (rarely ever with the faces) of their body parts and admiring them at my leisure — and none of them know. People find such behavior creepy — that I am having thoughts about strangers without them knowing, that I am creeping on them without them recognizing my creeping. But doesn't that define the nature of our intersubjectivity, of our mutuality on this planet? We creep on each other all the time, wondering about each other's lives, imagining what it's like to be someone else. At least it seems to me that that's what you do if you're not completely and narcissistically self-absorbed and are in any way remotely interested in the lives of other people.

Granted, not everyone creeps like I do. And I admit that I perhaps take my creepiness a step or two further than most. I remember following a young man around a museum. He was gorgeous, in short tight khaki shorts and a tight black t-shirt, his mop of hair begging for a hand to reach out and pull his head back a bit, revealing his pouty lips and full eyes. I never got close enough to see the color of them, but no matter: I enjoyed following him around, alone, wandering from room to room of modern art. What was he thinking as he stopped before a work of art? Was he admiring it? Was he wondering what the hell the artist was thinking? The ever receding doubleness of the experience increased my interest, me wandering while wondering what he was wondering about what an artist was imagining as he worked with those oils, as she arranged these items. But is this a receding, or a coming closer? Surely, I could've sidled up to him and engaged him in conversation, but how many times have I or you or any of us done that and been greeted with some skepticism, or even shock? It's hard to approach strangers. It's creepy if you don't do it just right. So maybe it's a little safer to creep and wonder, moving along with another human, trying to walk, if not in his shoes, at least near them, in his footsteps. The act of imagination here is what's important to me. Certainly, I snapped a pic of his cute little butt, the deliciously jutting curve of his behind answered by him raising his hand to his head, scratching an itch, or a fumbling toward a question with which any of us might identify: *What next? Why am I here?*

What the hell am I doing here?

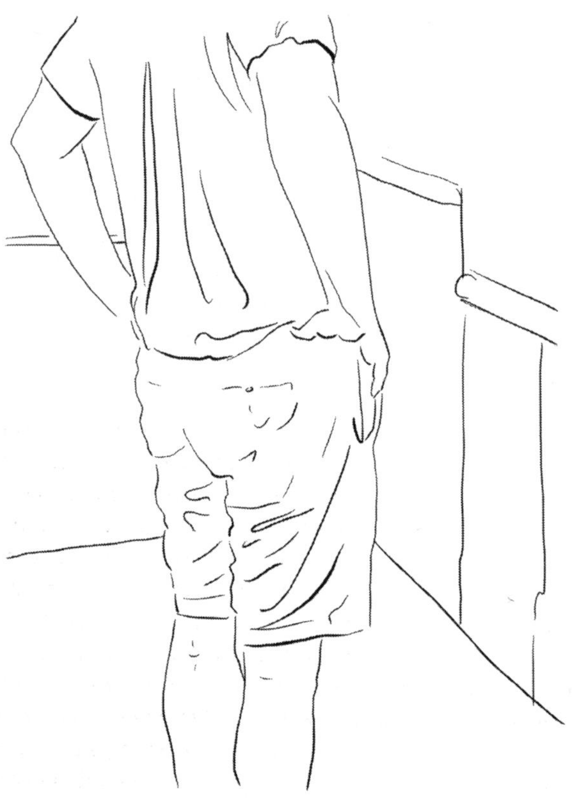

I know I am not the only one taking such covert pictures, and I'm sometimes creeped out myself by the thought of people taking such pictures of me. Though I hope they do. I'd be a little disappointed if no one ever did. I put on my tight gym shorts and tight black t-shirt and go get a coffee, sitting down to write this book, and hope that the hipster barista is checking out my ass as I walk away with my $4 coffee. I suspect he's not, but I have caught some glances at times. I totally wear these shorts because they are eye catching, perhaps because they're going to draw the eyes of that barista even if he doesn't want to look. Maybe that's even creepier than I really want to be. Or not. I recognize my male privilege in wearing clothing that's gaze-attracting, even as I can feel somewhat safe in my skin, knowing I'm not likely to be raped or attacked.

But at times I do feel the gaze as potentially hostile, and I wonder if the tightness in my shorts is perhaps just a little too snug. Am I asking for too much attention? And is the attention I'm getting not the kind I would want? That, after all, is the source of so much creepiness: *unwanted attention.* And yet I'm willing to take the risk in attracting it. You can meet some interesting people through it, have some chance encounters, however small or fleeting — or consequential. I think of Samuel Delany, writing at length in his critical memoir *Times Square Red, Times Square Blue*, about creeping on the poor and working class in old Times Square. He'd given them money for blowjobs, sure, but he also claims to have met some wonderful friends — folks he otherwise wouldn't have met.[3] I don't pursue sexual exchanges the way he did, but I do at times get compliments, get a comment on my computer bag or tattoo. Granted, not all attention is the attention I want, and the older women who scope me out don't creep me out, but I also don't encourage their stares. Just not what I

3 While I don't quote from this book, I feel compelled to cite it because it's something you should read: Samuel Delany, *Times Square Red, Times Square Blue* (New York: New York University Press, 1999).

want. But I accept that that's part of the deal. You present yourself and you understand that people will look.

I'm looking too.

The most interesting creeping I've experienced was once when, sitting in a pizza parlor waiting for my slice to be heated up, a young guy comes in to make an order. Just the kind of boy I like, standing straight up, his khaki shorts hugging his behind. I pretended to check messages on my phone and snapped a pic of his cute little ass. When I focused in on the picture later, zooming in and out to admire the curves of his glutes, I noticed another young man, slightly behind and to the side, looking straight at me taking a picture of this young man. I was totally creeped out. Did he catch me creeping? Did he know what I was doing? Or was he creeping *me*, not knowing at all that I was creeping this other young man? I'll never know, but I return to this picture often, wondering what he's thinking. He's totally cute: a bearded hipster with glasses. But beyond his physical appearance, what I love about him is his willingness to spy on me, his interest. If I'd known he was there, if I hadn't been as distracted by the other boy's ass, I might have looked back and smiled. Maybe.

Or maybe not. And this perhaps is the limit of creepiness. My creepiness and the creeping of others tells me that we are curious — but afraid. We look, but don't want to touch. And I generally don't — want to touch, that is. I'm not predatory in this behavior. I'm not looking for a sexual conquest. And when I'm creeped upon, I don't think others are necessarily thinking about sexually engaging me. We are intrigued. But we decline to make contact.

Is this a failure? Am I holding back? Oh totally. I don't want you to know how much of a creep I really am. Or we might get close, we might become friends, and then you might hurt me. Then again, in my own creepy way, perhaps the creepiest thing

I can do is leave you wondering why you've read this far, having invested this much time in my thinking about my creepiness.

Yes, to be sure, there are other limits to consider. Without a doubt, there's a gender dynamic to this that I have to acknowledge yet again. I can indulge my creepiness *in no small part because I'm a man.* Women who are creeped on in the way that I sometimes creep on young men are completely within their rights to feel not just creeped out but afraid and angry. They are subject to so much more actual attack than men are. So, I need to make some differentiations. I'm not talking about the kind of creeping that leads to stalking. In fact, I'd make a huge distinction between the creeping I'm describing and stalking. The former is an acknowledgment of interest and curiosity; the latter an imposition of damaged need and perverted desire. I can offer my apologia for creepiness; there is no such for stalking, which is simply predatory behavior that refuses to recognize the object of interest as capable of feeling or response or sovereignty. I came close to stalking Faith, the older woman who was my friend in college. But even I knew, creepy as I am, when to cut it out and back off.

Certainly, part of my creepiness is a fascination with youth, perhaps an attempt, however odd, to recover a sense of my own youth, my younger body. I want to see myself again as young and desirable. No, that's not right. I want to see myself as young and desirable *for the first time.* Of everything taken from me, that might be the thing I resent most: I never had a sense as a young person that I was desirable, that I could be desired, because I was too busy worrying over how my own desires were damning me to hell. When nearly every time you masturbate as a young person and you think this is the ejaculation that baptizes you into the Church of Satan, you can't help but feel fucked, damaged. So, I'm actually grateful for seeing those movie images of Tom Cruise dancing around in his underpants. They actually

still *move* me to this day. They showed me, however fleetingly and illicitly as my friend and I snuck into the rated-R movie, that there was a different way to relate to my body. I'm constantly recreating those images, taking pics of my own ass wiggling around, catching glimpses of others. I'm recreating that sense of the possible. Even now, I'm sitting here at Peet's next to a cute young guy, creeping him, but not enough to creep him out. Why don't I talk to him? Because I really fetishize *potential.* I look at these young people and want their lives, if only because my own youth was so taken from me.

I've worked out other ways to recreate my relationship to my body, to craft other scripts for me that try to repair the damages done. I have complex rituals, fantasies I attempt to enact that tell a different story about me, my body, my desires. They're almost all totally creepy, if only because they sexualize places in ways that aren't really meant to be sexualized, at least not the way I'm sexualizing them. Like snapping a pic of a guy's butt on the subway, I'm covertly making sexual a scene that isn't supposed to be. And if people start paying attention, they'd see what I'm doing. Sometimes I think they *do* see, but quietly participate in my creepiness.

But some places just seem to beg for creepiness. For me, the gym is one of the most powerful of such scenes. As a kid, PE classes were a constant site of trauma; I was awkward and ungainly, completely ill at ease in my body, a dis-ease made all the more palpable for me by the ceaseless taunts and ridicule of my peers. *What kind of pathetic faggot are you? Can't you even catch a fucking ball? We don't want that fucking faggot on our team.* Yes, I was the kid always chosen last. Correction: I was not chosen, but relegated to the team unfortunate to wind up with me because I had to go somewhere.

It took me a long time to feel—even remotely—comfortable in gym spaces. I avoided them for decades. But as I got older and started to put on weight, and as my joints sent signals that they were only ever going to become increasingly inflexible, I decided I needed to get over myself and start working out. I found a trainer willing to work with me and joined a gym. It was terrifying. Ok, perhaps I exaggerate a little bit — but only just a little. What helped me get over the panic, though, was the presence of numerous good-looking, often young bodies. While I'd never have looked openly while an adolescent, now, an older man, no one was looking at me, so they didn't seem particularly to care that I might be surreptitiously checking them out. They just weren't expecting it. Or if they did, they thought me harmless. Gratefully, I realized they weren't policing me, as I had been viciously policed in high school.

So, I checked them out. And loved it. A young guy gets onto the treadmill next to me and I can breathe in his masculine energy. A guy next to me bends over to lift his weights and I can check out the taut curves of his butt. I eventually began to look forward to going to the gym to see these young buff bodies, some regulars whom I anticipated seeing, but always surprised by new flesh. And then the trainers themselves became an interesting object of scrutiny. I was surprised by how often they — always young men I chose to train me — had to touch me, to correct postures, to adjust positions, to help me feel the muscles they were trying to isolate for attention. I'd go once, then twice, sometimes three times a week so I could feel their hands on my body. By this point, I already had a lover, even a husband, but I couldn't help but thrill to the touch of these young muscled hands, correcting me, massaging me, guiding my body in ways they wanted.

Could they feel my pleasure in their touch? Did they feel it themselves? Of course, no one talked about it. And therein lay part of the pleasure of the scene for me: here were bodies touching, certainly in ritualized and pre-scripted ways, but touching nonetheless. Here was a man, I'm sure always straight, helping me help my body — and always by touching it, stroking muscles, caring for my body. I had paid them to do so, surely, but they were attentive to my body in ways that I never had been. They delighted when I lost weight. They praised my growing biceps. They chided if I confessed about eating that early morning donut. They wanted me to want a better body, a stronger body, a body that another man could praise openly in this once, to me, immensely hostile space.

I was transfixed by their interest. I felt myself transforming, in body and mind.

We never talked about relationships. I suppose that these trainers were all schooled *not* to get personal with their clients. I respected that boundary, never offering personal details but also never inquiring. I didn't really want to know about them. And I frankly didn't want them to know about me. I felt they might touch me less, or differently, if they knew I was queer. I preferred to keep it, in a word, creepy. At least in my own mind. I was just getting too much out of it, in body and mind.

And wow, could it be creepy—but deliciously so. I remember seeing a dude at the gym carrying a belt with chains. What the fuck is that for? A trainer took me to the TRX machine, a complex system of ropes with handles and metal loops. I couldn't help but think of this as a large restraining device, out in the open, the trainer, my master, putting me through my paces. At his instruction, I'd grasp the handles, wrapping the ropes around my wrist, strapping myself into the machine, while he'd bend down to whisper in my ear, "Get it up, squeeze that ass." I'd go down again and again into a squat. If I didn't put enough weight on my heels to support myself, or if I didn't go down far enough, he'd lightly swat my upper thigh. "Get it up, squeeze that ass." I'd work harder and harder, wanting to feel that swat, and he'd reward me with the strangest of gym lover's talk: "I love it when you drip," my sweat flinging off my forehead when I moved from one set of ropes to another, doing a circuit of deliciously painful exercises that I ultimately came to crave as much for the resulting endorphin release as for any touch of my trainer's hand.

My favorite trainer, with whom I worked out for two years, would tell me –if I had to be away for a week or so– that he missed me. He'd do a little jig while we worked out, excited by my progress, caressing my biceps as they steadily grew, putting me in the upright pushup position for a couple of minutes if I fibbed on myself about a carb I shouldn't have had. I wanted both his praise and his censure. I wanted him at times to punish me. I'd walk into the gym and literally ask to be punished. I wanted a hard session. I wanted to drip. I wanted him to love it when I dripped. One of his co-workers, a young woman, would look at me, then look at him, and say something like: "He only dances when you are here." Perhaps she was playfully teasing him, but I couldn't help but think to myself, how dare she make him self-conscious about our time together. For of course, I figured that, if he knew how much I got off on our time together, he'd turn away. Maybe. I don't know. We were never intimate in any way that wasn't perfectly visible to all in the gym. I never talked about my husband. To be fair, I never jerked off to this guy either. But I loved, if not him, then our time together sweating. And I frankly relished the tension between what I imagined happening and what was really happening. That's perhaps the creepy part, the part that generates creepiness: we were doing something that was perfectly normal to anyone looking in, but there was always the possibility that one of us, namely me, could be interpreting it in completely inappropriate ways. That is, I could be eroticizing something that, for him and for probably most everyone else in the gym, wasn't really supposed to be erotic.

Or was it? I don't know, honestly. There is the delicious perversity of the sauna, people assembling post-workout to relax for a few minutes, to sweat together. I ogle a near naked boy flexing himself in the heat, removing his shorts in a full display — *wanting to display* — his chiseled torso, his emerging abs, his finely sculpted arms. Who couldn't imagine this as anything but a call to admire a tight young body? I do, even as I recognize the limits of desired articulation; an approach would be unwelcome, but admiring glances not. What qualifies as creepy here?

Surely, at times, lines are crossed. Craigslist is full of ads for guys looking for hook ups in the shower stalls of gyms, or "missed connections" with one guy asking another, one he's been eyeing in the weight room, if he too has been checking guys out, if perhaps he might have noticed himself being admired. I never hooked up with a guy in a gym. But I had one trainer for a bit, just a couple of months, who could tell I was totally into the gym as a scene of punishment, that I understood the gym as not just a space to discipline my body but to play out fantasies of being a young tough stud working out with other tough studs. I didn't perform well on one challenge when we were alone one night at the gym, and he slapped my ass, hard, when I stood up. I totally jerked off to that scene when I got home. The trainer and I never talked openly about it, and he had to move away shortly after, but he could tell that my interest in the gym was complex, and he was willing to offer something of a helping hand.

I have no doubt I could have more such experiences if I sought them out. There's part of me that is surely deeply masochistic, that would delight in such punishment. Even returning to the gym every week is a form of masochism, given how often gyms were sites of tortured encounters and bullying for me as a child. I recreate the scenes of pain the better perhaps to control them, perhaps even master and overcome them, even as I still, to this day, think of myself as fully deserving punishment.

But I have also come to think that the creepiness of the gym doesn't emanate from just me. At the most basic level, the gym, with all of its ropes and weights and chains and grunts and people checking each other out, is actually in the service of making people more erotic, to each other and to themselves. Surely, exercising in the gym is about being healthy. But isn't it also, like so many other parts of our culture, about remaking bodies more enticing? About fitting into particular norms of appeal or attraction? I admit wanting to be more attractive physically, even as what drove me to the gym was a need to ease the creaking in my joints and to stop the ever-expanding belly from ripping my pants in two. But I won't lie: I loved slipping on my favorite nylon gym shorts, feeling my ass tone as I did my squats, checking out the studs sweating and grunting next to me. I can't be the only one.

I've come to think the gym is saturated with a kind of fundamental creepiness, a split between what people are ostensibly there to do and what they secretly hope will happen. Many of us are not just taking care of our bodies — and that we surely are doing, and it feels good to take care of one's body, especially when one had been taught for so long and so powerfully not only to disregard the body but to understand it as the source of sin, as that which must necessarily be denied. We also recognize the space for the scene of semi-erotic exchange it is — and for some people it is so very explicitly. More particularly for me, I'm both taking care of my body and making very queer — and creepily queer — a space that isn't supposed to be queer, that isn't supposed to be about open homoeroticism, however homosocial it is, with men touching each other and praising, however competitively, their progress.

Do I return to the gym, a scene of past shame and fear, in order to be acknowledged — but now on my own terms? Do I eroticize these times to repair them through play? Do I submit to the punishment — but am now the one calling the shots, paying the trainer who has to please me, ultimately, to keep his job? I now control how I am hurt. Nishant Shahani, in *Queer Retrosexualities*, argues that "It is not the affective state of shame that is, in itself, reparative. But it is its shared memory, transformed in retrospect that marks the reparative possibilities of shame for queer thinking."[4] Maybe so. Maybe I am recreating scenes from

4 Nishant Shahani, Queer Retrosexualities: The Politics of Reparative Return (Bethlehem, PA: Lehigh University Press, 2012), 19.

a collective shared memory—that banishment of the little faggot from the scene of manly camaraderie—but doing so in ways that allow me to control better what happens. I suppose a full queering of the gym would make the objects and trajectories of my homoerotic desire very palpable, would confront these buff boys with the homoeroticism of the gym itself. I'm not sure I'm doing that. In fact, I know I'm not. I'm doing something creepier. I'm allowing the secret of the homoerotic to stand, but insisting I can enjoy it anyway. I don't fool myself into thinking that I now belong in this place. But I permit myself the delicious perversity of enjoying it, and frankly of using this space and these trainers to facilitate my pleasure, even as I refrain from naming out loud what it is to me.

Ultimately, I make no promises about the uses to which I will put my body; I don't improve it to be a better worker, to reduce my future health care costs. No, I seek out the gym to feel myself a tough sexy fucker, to eye openly other men, to feel the touch of men in care for my body. I seek out the gym to experience everything I was denied as a boy, an adolescent—the right to feel my body as desirable, as worthy of care.

I know that my description of this might be creepy to some reading this. But I suspect it's a creepiness that even the trainers, and not just the one who swatted my ass, participate in. Or is it the prerogative of the creep to rationalize his creepiness by imagining his desires as shared by those around him? I know I rationalize; any apologia is perhaps more rationalization than not.

☙

Rationalizations aside, if we've learned anything in the foregoing exploration of creepiness, it's that creepiness is certainly situational, and what marks one as creepy at a particular time and place might strike another as simple eccentricity or even normal behavior in another. What I do that might strike some as creepy, the various stories I've told here, may just as well strike some others as, well, all too human and ordinary. Patterns and possibilities of creepiness emerge in a variety of places, and it is surprising how often we can mark such patterns, unsettling to me at times how often I have marked them in myself. We all judge ourselves. And the judge, jury, and executioner, when not realized in actual institutions meting out punishment for actual crimes, are still all powerfully present internally. But they are also present throughout the culture, sometimes in subtle ways re-enforcing norms.

J.R. Ackerley, and even Adam Kotsko, might have explored varieties of creepiness as a way, if not necessarily to normalize them, then at least to understand them, perhaps even invite our sympathy. Such emotional reorientation around creepiness is rare, though. In fact, two recent films I've been obsessed with, *While We're Young* and *The Overnight*, each pick up the specter of the creep with the possibility of salvaging him but ultimately re-assert normative family ties and identities. Perhaps unsurprisingly, given how many times we've seen the creep appear vis-à-vis families, these engaging and often hysterically funny movies begin with married couples, a little bit dissatisfied, each looking for something different. *While We're Young* concerns a middle-aged couple courted by and becoming intimately (if not sexually) involved with a younger couple, while *The Overnight* moves us to think about swinging and hints at polyamory as a lifestyle.[5] Both films invite viewers to gawk a bit — to creep on? — and perhaps poke some fun at urban hipster youth, even as they attempt to appeal to that viewership. But they also push us into somewhat unexpected and often unexplored intimate territory that gets, well, creepy.

---

5 Both films, while flawed, are worth seeing, if only for the discussions they might provoke: Noah Baumbach (dir.), *While We're Young*, Scott Rudin Productions, 2015; Patrick Brice (dir.), *The Overnight*, Duplass Brothers Productions, 2015.

Specifically, the movies probe the boundaries of what marriage is and speak to a simple truth: two people cannot be everything to each another. We need others. Or we are at least interested in others, even if not always sexually. Marital complexity isn't new to American cinema, and many dramas play out the difficulties of legalized coupledom. I was traumatized by *Kramer vs. Kramer* as a kid, wondering what would happen if my parents divorced, and I thought *Fatal Attraction* a dire warning in my young adulthood about the dangers of cheating. And more recently, *Fifty Shades of Grey*, however tepidly, offered its own spin on different kinds of "contractual" relations. But the complexities of intimacy— especially the opening up of a relationship to include others— is rarely coded as not creepy in some fundamental way in much of this pop culture film—hence *Fatal Attraction* and *Fifty Shades*.

But to their credit, these films try. In fact, as excited as I am (as a queer man) about the 2015 Supreme Court decision that expands marriage rights nationwide to lesbians and gays, I'm almost more intrigued by the questioning of marriage offered by *While We're Young* and The Overnight. Along such lines, many viewers will find much to relate to in these films. In Noah Baumbach's While We're Young, middle-aged Josh (Ben Stiller) and Cornelia Srebnick (Naomi Watts) seem to have a good if somewhat staid life in New York, Josh having hit something of a dead end in his documentary film career. His big and baggy film about a leftist intellectual is overlong and going nowhere. Enter a young couple, Jamie (Adam Driver) and Darby Massey (Amanda Seyfried). Jamie presents himself to Josh after one of the latter's classes, claiming to be a fan of his work. The couples go out to dinner, and the older pair is clearly charmed by the younger duo's seemingly creative approach to life. The foursome participates, for instance, in a drug-infused ayahuasca ceremony, projectile vomiting their way to supposedly insight-bearing hallucinations. Jamie and Cornelia make out a little bit in this extended scene, but it's all in good fun (for now).

In subsequent hangouts, we see and share with Josh and Cornelia the discreet charms of the young—their retro sensibilities (playing actual board games, not computer games; buying vinyl, not MP3s) and art- and pleasure-focused life. They're invigorating, as the young often are. And as Jamie is an aspiring filmmaker, Josh has a chance to play at being a mentor to someone who seems genuinely interested in his (otherwise forgotten) films. Something of a bromance blooms between the two, and we wonder where this all will lead, particularly as Josh begins to adopt the attire and manners of the younger man, while also constantly picking up the check for dinners and drinks out.

On the other side of the continent, in Patrick Brice's *The Overnight*, Alex (Adam Scott) and Emily (Taylor Schilling) are young marrieds with child who have just moved to Los Angeles, lamenting that they not only don't have any friends in the area but also are unsure how –in their post-college 20s– to go about making friends. Enter Kurt (Jason Schwartzman) and Charlotte (Judith Godrèche), a flashy couple to the rescue. Kurt meets Adam and Emily in a park after discovering that their young sons have hit it off and enjoy playing together. Kurt invites the new-to-town couple over, and a lovely dinner turns into an overnight of skinny-dipping, pot-smoking, and soul-baring bonding. Kurt and Charlotte are the wealthier versions of Jamie and Darby in *While We're Young*, but no less arty; Kurt has a studio where he paints pictures of sphincters. We also see a bit of early bromance as the overly endowed Kurt helps Alex deal with his feeling of penile inadequacy. The presence of cocks on screen (however prosthetic) signals an increasing sexualization of the evening, which ramps up when Charlotte takes Emily on a booze run that turns into a trip to a massage parlor so Emily can peep through a hole while Charlotte gives an impromptu hand job. We wonder where this adult slumber party might be headed.

What's particularly compelling about these films is the frankness with which male–male intimacies are treated. Josh and Jamie's intergenerational bromance acts in a surrogate father/son or big bro/little bro fashion for the two, but it's not without its complexity. We see the two in deep conversation with one another, often over meals on "man dates." In a twist, Josh comes to envy Jamie's creativity, the mentoring relationship flipping a bit, and the portrayal of their friendship risks some complexity as they seem both intimate and competitive at the same time — perhaps an inevitable combination in male bonding in American capitalist society. There's nothing overtly sexual here, but it's clear that Josh needs the younger man, just as much as Jamie needs Josh's mentoring and connections. In *The Overnight*, Kurt helps Alex "come out" about how much he doesn't like his body (especially his penis size). At one point, the wives stumble across Kurt photographing Alex sexily wriggling his butt, and we wonder with them what exactly guys actually do when they are alone together. But they are getting to know one another, and Kurt's ease in his own body translates into a jock-like encouragement to Alex, as though he's coaching his player to get back in the game of self-confidence and strut his stuff. Kurt engineers a "show" for the ladies so Alex can show off his manhood. These are intimate moments between men. And curiously, they come after all of the men are married. In watching these interactions, I couldn't help but think of *I Love You, Man*, the 2009 film that tracked the emergence of the bromance into mainstream culture. But in that film, the bromance occurs before the marriage — in fact, it must occur before the marriage. We get the sense that our hero, Peter, has to pass through the gauntlet of learning how to relate to a buddy before he can mature into a coupled relationship with a woman. The heterosexual path is maturing from relations with your friends to your spouse. *While We're Young* and *The Overnight* flip the script, showing the power and potential of male–male intimacies within a heterosexual marriage. I can't help but wonder what's changed in the past several years, if not perhaps greater queer visibility prompting greater comfort with a wider variety of male–male intimacies.

Both films are played for lots of laughs, especially *The Overnight*, which can be hysterical, even if at times creepily uncomfortable with its frank portrayal of straight guys trying to figure out how to flirt with one another. And they both nicely foreground, without too much recourse to stereotype, the attractions of young hipster culture, however achingly white and privileged. But each movie also turns a bit serious, as comedies do, before resolving the tensions created by the couples' newfound intimacies. In *While We're Young*, we learn that Jamie has essentially engineered his meeting with Josh to get closer to Josh's famous father-in-law, a leading documentarian of his generation. Jamie has ambitions, and he's not beyond using others — and Josh's (Platonic midlife crisis) interest in him — to get what he wants. In fact, Jamie's fabrications are creepily extraordinary. He's concocted not only his friendship with Josh but the subject matter of his own documentary — an irony given the "truth-telling" ethos implicit in documentary work. But no one but Josh seems bothered by this. And when Josh confronts Jamie about both his professional and personal deceptions — a somewhat ludicrous if still pathos-driven declaration of hurt: "I loved you," followed by Jamie's "I really liked you" — we are left wondering where the truth in any relationship might be. To borrow from a filmic metaphor, such truths are perhaps mostly the projections we cast on each other, needing others to perform roles in our different dramas. Josh is certainly left wondering what needs he tried to fill through his friendship with the younger man.

Meanwhile, *The Overnight* ramps up to fever pitch, and just as the foursome is about to call it a night, we learn that Kurt and Charlotte are trying to spice up their now-defunct sex life by swinging a bit, with Kurt particularly interested in Alex. All this comes after Alex and Emily have a movingly painful and honest conversation in the bathroom about how, as committed as they are to each another, they nonetheless think of others, sexually and intimately. A little bit of truth goes a long way to mutual understanding. And just as the party is about to break up, all four wind up in bed together, starting with a group hug leading to the boys kissing one another. The silent soundtrack (a little bit of fleshly slurping aside) is comically interrupted by the two little boys bursting into the bedroom wanting breakfast. Alex and Emily flee, and the night, now morning, ends in a hungover walk of shame, but still funny.

While We're Young and *The Overnight* move us toward ways of talking about such needs and possibilities, such necessary extra-marital relations. But traditionally, comedies end in marriage. Conflicts are resolved, love secured, and all is now right with the world, at least for the time being. But what's often most interesting in a comedy is less the expected resolution than the complications encountered along the way—complications that can suggest possibilities of unhappy endings, but also alternative paths forsaken. With both *While We're Young* and *The Overnight,* I couldn't help but think of those forsaken paths of desire, and I ultimately regretted the easy ends both films make of tough loves. Predictably, the films exhibit a failure of nerve to follow through in helping us imagine capacious alternatives, new trajectories for sustainable and nurturing relations with others. *The Overnight* ends with the two couples running into each other in the park where Kurt first met Alex and Emily; the meeting, initially awkward, quickly turns bathetic as the two couples comment about how their adventuresome evening led them to reaffirm their commitments to one another as spouses. Kurt and Charlotte are even in therapy. At the end of *While We're Young,* we see Josh and Cornelia about to catch a plane a year or so later, having had their own child in the interim. The answer for them is simple: get your own kid, not someone else's.

Curiously, children haunt both films. In *The Overnight* they sleep in the background, waiting to remind the adults to stop playing around, while having a child is the ultimate answer to the problem of growing older and feeling old before your time in *While We're Young.* Indeed, what I find most challenging about both films is the shadowy presence of kids, who are often asleep in both movies. They may slumber, but they are stark calls to remember what a "normal" marriage is: the serious business of child production. That's a lot of pressure for two people, who often have multiple and divergent interests. Perhaps, after all, child rearing is too much to ask of just two people — but neither film goes there, even if each falls back on the presence of children to assure the return to normalcy and the happy ending of (therapized) marital bliss. And the heteronormative is reaffirmed.

I'm not surprised, ultimately, at the end of either film, and I often chide myself for expecting too much from these corporately produced entertainments, however "indie" they are. For both films, the moral is clear: reaffirm the marriage, hunker down with your spouse, and make your own damn family. At a time when the right to marry has just been extended in this country, we have a unique opportunity to think collectively about what a marriage is — and perhaps about how much pressure we have put on the institution of marriage. If anything, we might read these two films as anxious questionings about the limits of marriage to satisfy our needs, both for sexual intimacy and for family. We're letting more kinds of people get married now — a good thing, surely — but perhaps these films are generating some (nervous?) laughter about the limits of marriage itself. And while the comedic genre might traditionally end with valuing the bonds of marriage, these funny, poignant films at least pose interesting thought experiments about the inability of marriage to fulfill all our needs, much less address our curiosities. The fact that these films are showing us heterosexual couples confronting the boundaries of their relationships is telling. Perhaps the queering of marriage might offer new possibilities for thinking about such questions, for entertaining more interesting thought experiments.

Such entertaining requires that we risk creepy territory, that we give ourselves permission to probe creepiness. I must admit, as someone who has worked as a college teacher for over 20 years and is now solidly middle-aged, I found *While We're Young* a bit painfully — and creepily — close to my life at times. I've had some wonderful friendships with former students, little brothers and sisters who have energized and reinvigorated me professionally and personally— as well as one such friendship with a young man that, while not at all predatory like the one depicted in *While We're Young*, ended with an inability to manage expectations and projections. Shit happens. Similarly, the odd threesomes and foursomes of my 20s comprised my own personal version of *The Overnight*. Now queerly married, the one thing I know about marriage is that my husband, as wonderful as he is, is a huge part of my life—but a *part*. We both need others, even if not necessarily sexually. And childless, we have learned there are many ways to make a "family," not just biologically. My dearest friend Karen, whom I refer to as my non-sexual life partner; my best straight and married friend Michael, who has identified our relationship as a kind of romance and who so wanted to hold my hand during a pride parade; my former student David, who is so like the son I never had but always wanted, who texts me pictures of himself on his various journeys and adventures to let me know what he's doing, that he's ok—all are terribly dear to me. But also, my gym trainer, and also perhaps the boys whose butts I snap pictures of.

Such queer family building is something that many gays are adept at, and the possibility of sexual plurality in gay relationships is something that I take as part of my gay inheritance, a bit of being in the world that, while not unknown amongst straights, is more culturally supported amongst many gays of my generation. I could, for instance, contrast the foregoing two films with Edmund White's story of his sexual experiences in *My Lives*. White isn't afraid to detail his sexual exploits, his extramarital obsessions, even when they border on the particularly creepy. Indeed, while mainstream film curtails the creep, queer culture, I contend, finds ways to embrace them at times—not always, and not evenly, but definitely more so than normative straight culture, and with few apologies.

Published in 2006, with the author well into his 60s, *My Lives* focuses dominantly, if not almost exclusively, on the author's sexual exploits. In chapters variously describing "My Hustlers" and "My Blonds," White recounts one sexual episode after another, his experiences ranging from numerous one-night stands to relationships of different durations, frequently punctuated with affairs and occasional group sex. Even more innocuously titled chapters — "My Shrinks," "My Europe," and even "My Mother" and "My Father" — are laced throughout with sex, sex, sex.

One stunning chapter, late in the book, "My Master," recounts a sadomasochistic affair between the author, who's 60, and a man in his early 20s. White describes being whipped, tied, fucked, and pissed on by this young man, called "T," who introduced himself initially as a fan of White's work but soon became the elder man's object of obsessive sexual interest. Recounting the height of this passion, White tells us, "Now my life was full, purposeful, directed: every waking moment was aimed at T."[6] White's interest in "T," compared to past liaisons, takes a particularly compulsive turn, and the author obsessively clings to "T," especially when he feels the younger man is growing bored with the relationship and wanting to move on to set up house with someone closer to his own age. White repeatedly emails and calls the younger man, who ultimately puts additional distance between White and himself to ward off the burden of White's desires and emotional investment. White is hardly blind to his own compulsive and creepy behavior here; in fact, he seems to revel in it. The chapter is filled with both self-mockery and pathos, constantly blurring into one another. On one hand, he shows us his post-"T" self, riddled with self-hatred, cruising web ads for hookups all night long; we see him "clicking on the computer and tapping out obscene messages, an old man with a belly hanging in the sling of his T-shirt, sitting for hours and hours in his underpants, bare feet getting cold from the air sluicing in through the badly insulated window."[7] On the other hand, such self-mockery turns pathetic in his realization that "It

6 Edmund White, *My Lives: A Memoir* (New York: Ecco, 2006), 255.

7 Ibid., 256.

did seem so unfair to me that we could have had sex a hundred eighty times together over twenty-six months and then one fine day he could decide unilaterally, almost as a whim, that it was all over."[8]

White's fiction has always skirted the line between the imaginative and the memoir, but his outpouring of work in the late 2000s—including the novel *Married Man*, the stories in the collection *Chaos*, and the memoir of his youth in *City Boy*—signals a ramping up, as it were, of a seeming need to "tell all," and quickly. White himself seems aware that his drive to narrate, whether under the guise of barely disguised fiction or in lurid autobiography, has become, well, a bit creepy. Within the context of narrating "My Master," he painfully recounts his own drive to narrate the events as they unfolded, not just in retrospect: "I told everyone."[9] And he does, telling the sordid tale to anyone who will listen—friends, family, colleagues at Princeton, even his partner since 1995, Michael Carroll, to whom he turns to help him lick his wounds when suffering "T"'s various blows and rebuffs, literally and figuratively. Such narrative compulsion becomes self-reflexively thematized in the text as White imagines his friends reading the chapter on "My Master" and thinking "TMI"—"too much information." But then the passage moves quickly to a recounting of yet another perverse sex scene and White's feelings of being inadequate to the task of serving his demanding young master. In reflecting on the book and this chapter in particular, White confesses that

> While writing it I knew perfectly well that, especially in chapters like "My Master," I would be leading the usual reader too far, dangerously deep into the realm of the perverse, but I was willing to take that risk: I wanted to sound like a regular guy who turns out to be seriously eccentric, the passenger beside

8 Ibid.
9 Ibid., 257.

> you in the plane who seems boringly normal until his talk takes an unsettling turn.[10]

And he succeeds. He often creeps us out.

Critical reaction to *My Lives* has been at times unflattering with reviewers complaining that it is "obsessive" and lacking in depth, often "equating […] human complexity with a handful of words." At best, according to Peter Conrad in *The Guardian*, "*My Lives* is a saga of picaresque promiscuity, a Satyricon of satyriasis" in which "homosexuality is central […] treated as something heroic but also obsessional and at times degrading."[11] In general, critics seem to lose patience with White's sexual antics. As White himself puts it, "The book as it stands is heavy on sex and light on intellectual adventure or artistic retrospection."[12] But I must admit that the sex White recounts is never boring; an armchair psychoanalyst (and White positions you as just such a reader at times) would have a field day here, particularly with White's recounting of the closeness of his relationship to his mother and his rather distant and disapproving father. But the sense I get from the critics is that White's sexual behavior seems childish, and that a man his age should really (fucking) know better. Even a colleague of mine in Women's Studies complained, after hearing me give a talk about White's work, that White seemed like a troll. Why won't he just grow up?

In a word, why does he have to be such a *creep*?

I'm attracted, I admit, to the creep in all of these folks — in Edmund White, in the Ben Stiller character, in Ackerley and his search for an ideal friend. None of my experiences with folks

10 This and the following quotations by White are taken from an addendum to the Ecco edition of *My Lives,* which includes interviews with the author and other commentary. Ibid., 7.

11 Peter Conrad, "An Oral History," *The Guardian,* Sept. 17, 2005, http://www.guardian.co.uk/books/2005/sep/18/biography.features.

12 White, *My Lives,* 13.

have bordered on anything like that described by White, and I'm almost a little envious of the author and his bold forays into truly creepy territory. He allowed himself a connection, however unusual, however unconventional, however open to the judgment of those around him and those reading him that he might just in fact be a real live creep. I'll likely never go as far as White does, but I respect the desire to cross some boundaries, to risk a certain creepiness, in the pursuit of knowing others, even reclaiming a bit of a lost youth — or a youth never had.

❧

Perhaps we are all creeps sometime. I'd like to think I know when to stop, when I've perhaps gone a bit too far, or am about to. I could tell you, for instance, about J., a barista at one of the coffee shops where I do most of my morning writing. (We've been here before, if you remember.) He's a nice kid, in his 30s, exactly the kind of boy who gets my attention: not too cute, perhaps a little intense, but not all that much really. It's the hipster drag, the beard and flannel, the rough looking pants that make him look prickly, when, in fact, he's actually a very nice man: wanting to engage in conversation, share restaurant recommendations, inform you about the $7 coffee you're drinking, and wish you a very pleasant morning.

In a moment of weakness (his), he confessed some personal trouble one morning, a need to move quickly out of his current apartment and find another. He confessed that such was only part of his larger fears for his future as he was past 30 and still slinging coffee, in however a high-price fashion. He needed a career, but found himself fumbling. I was moved. I carry with me various greeting cards, a minor occupational hazard as a handwritten "thank you" or "thinking of you" often goes a long way to making someone's day and thus keeping my large network vibrant. I took one out and wrote him a note, saying, no, I wasn't coming on to him, I am in fact married, but I was concerned,

I'm a teacher, working with a lot of young people, and invited him to email or text me to talk more about his situation.

Weeks passed, and I thought that I couldn't show my face there again. I'd done something truly creepy. I'd left a note, with contact information, to a stranger—a male stranger at that. I debated within myself, all of the voices of creepiness clamoring for attention. How weird could I be? At best, you're just a fool. But then again, what's wrong with reaching out? His may have been, as I've characterized it, a moment of weakness, but he nonetheless reached out himself, if only momentarily. Why not reach back? But really, what a creep I am. How can he not read my note as anything but a gesture, a potentially unwanted probing of sexual interest? After all, I was just a tiny bit attracted to him. I'd asked after the boots he was wearing once, where'd he get them, did he like them, while wondering, purely in the twisted halls of my own fantasy, if he'd like me to lick them clean, scuffed as they were. But seriously, that was just a passing thought. I'm not going to engage him sexually. Perhaps I could be a friend. I like helping young people. I like helping young *men*, particularly *young* men, because of my own damaged "youth." I sound pathetic. I don't even sound as confident as Edmund White, just abjectly prostrating himself to his desires for young male flesh.

So, I avoided the coffee shop, coming close only once while walking around the consumer plaza where I'd once felt somewhat comfortable. I wasn't there by accident. I went one late afternoon practically daring myself to get close, just to sneak a peek through the windows to see if he was there. I walked through the maze of hipster shops, even daring to pass by the shop, only with the stealthiest of glances in. Fuck, I'm stalking. I'd already googled the coffee shop, which has a ton of Instagram pictures, looking for this guy, to see if he was in any picture. No luck. Another week, I'm not hearing anything, and I'm confident he's told everyone in the coffee shop that I'm the creepiest of creeps, this old guy who left him a card, silly old faggot.

And then he texts. A long, lovely message about how he's sorry he didn't get back in touch, he's been meaning to write, he's just been so busy with the move, but my card made his day, maybe his week, and he'd love to get together for a drink or a coffee or lunch, because, after all, you can never have too many "good" friends. That's what he wrote: "good" in quotation marks, just like that. And I spent fifteen minutes wondering what "good" means. I texted back and invited him over for a drink that night, and he couldn't, of course, already had plans. But in time, we had a burger at the hipster bar near my house and we started to get to know one another. He's a nice guy, a little lost, but trying, maybe not trying too hard.

And that was that. Further attempts to get together just didn't happen, although he always responded politely to my texts, claiming he wanted to get together but always had something else going on. I resumed visits to the coffee shop, and he was never anything less than pleasant. I became more formal and stiff, feeling rebuffed. I once even purposefully engaged another barista in friendly banter, laughing loudly at our shared jokes about a $7 cup of coffee that just wasn't quite worth it, and hahahaha before turning to my formerly potential friend and paying for my drink with a stone-cold face.

In writing this out, I realize that here is the real creepiness. Nothing creepy in asking to be friends. But perhaps a bit creepy in punishing someone for not trying as hard as I wanted. Or for saying no by putting me off, however gently. For just needing, for whatever his reasons, to put his energy somewhere else. And I inevitably think of my father, who put his energy somewhere, but rarely into me. And of my uncle, who didn't live long enough to parent me in ways I can only imagine in retrospect. And various friends who are busy with their own lives. And while I wanted to hold this young man accountable for all of the ways in which I'd been robbed of my youth, I knew I needed to turn away and leave him alone.

Have you liked where I've taken you? Have I creeped you out? Have you perhaps creeped yourself out in having read this far? I've enjoyed the reactions when I've told people that I'm writing a book called Creep. I get off on their perplexity, even confusion. *Surely, Jonathan, what do you know about being a creep? You seem so nice, so successful, so put together.*

But creepiness is a long-term relationship. Even at 50 I'm trying to figure out how to use it, lest I be used by it. It's a tricky balance. And I wonder if my story here has only been a generational accounting, its lessons, such as they are, nontransferable across the decades. Maybe my particular creepiness, cultivated in the hot mess of the homophobic deep south of the 1970s is a special thing — one that, hopefully, fewer and fewer will have to experience. But still, I can't help but think that we are all driven by some demons, and, even if you make friends with them, they are still demons. Surely, at times they can teach, even guide. You just might not always like where they take you.

And as I've suggested, sometimes I think we can be creepy in *critical* ways, or at least I fool myself into thinking such a thing is possible. Come with me, back to New Orleans, the scene of so many crimes, and not just against me and my kind. One more story of creeping before I let you go. One more attempt to make an apologia for what I've become.

It's late March, just past midday, a bit humid, but not unbearably so. I'm about to board a van with a bunch of strangers who have all signed up for a Katrina tour, a three-hour survey of the devastating floods that submerged ninety percent of the city in the aftermath of the hurricane and the failure of the levee system. Folks from New Jersey, Illinois, and even Canada talk excitedly about water damage and urban blight. Almost 10 years to the day and the floods still fascinate.

Besides our guide, I'm the only one from New Orleans. I was born and raised here, but I'm not telling anyone. I'm undercover, a closeted native. I want to experience the tour as a visitor, a stranger, as someone whose family wasn't impacted by Katrina and the flooding (even though we were, dramatically). I want some distance. Or maybe I want to erase the distance I have felt from this place; to remember, to reflect, to live all of it again. But I definitely want to *creep* up on the place, perhaps take it unawares. Approaching the ten-year anniversary of the event, I want to feel my way again, toward which memories are important. As you now know, I left New Orleans over twe nty years ago; a queer man struggling with his sexuality in the Deep South, I needed to leave to find myself in less hostile places. I'm torn. This has been home and not home. I wonder — after time, the storm, the flooding, the blood in the water — what it can be to me now. Regardless, I still feel a little creepy not outing myself as a native, if no longer a local. I'm, yet again, in disguise, hiding, peering out. I'm creeping.

The tour is one of many you can get in and around NOLA, with visits to the French Quarter and old plantations just upriver being some of the most popular. I am surprised that Katrina tours are still so in demand. I had to call around to a couple of places before finding an empty seat in a van that accommodates about 12. I get to ride shotgun with the tour guide, a guysy guy in a Saints ball cap, a native New Orleanian, someone I could've gone to high school with in Metairie, the large suburb to the west, just over the 17th Street Canal. He's been a guide for well over a decade and knows his stuff, winding the van through the old city's small streets, up Canal, around the French Quarter (streets closed for one of the many outdoor music fests), and into the Faubourg Marigny, one of the oldest neighborhoods near downtown. He jokes throughout the tour and is particularly playful with the kids on the van, testing their knowledge of historical events. But a certain seriousness lurks in the background. Constant reminders of flood levels, references to famous buildings that no longer exist, details of renovations undertaken since the waters receded. We can't go into the lower Ninth Ward apparently. According to our guide, city officials have put the area on a "no tour" list. Some of the wood used in the Brad Pitt homes (Pitt's Make It Right organization built over a hundred sustainable homes in the area) is apparently rotting, not having been treated to withstand the abundant moisture in the area. (Pitt's foundation is suing the supplier.)

While most of the afternoon focuses on Katrina, our guide weaves in some other local color, particularly the famous aboveground tombs. When your city is largely six-plus feet below sea level, you don't bury people in the ground. We pull over to walk around an old cemetery, dates in the family vaults stretching way back into the 18th century. As new generations pass, old remains are swept to the back and fall to the bottom, piling on top of one another over the years.

Thinking of the dust of generations easily recalls scenes from almost exactly a decade ago. My sister called on a Sunday, sobbing into the phone, just days after the storm and reports of the flooding were being televised nonstop. My dad wouldn't live much longer. He'd been suffering from Parkinson's for well over a decade, his health slowly deteriorating. The last year had been particularly rough, the physical and cognitive debilitation having taken a sharp turn for the worse. I had visited earlier in the summer, at my mother's insistence, to give her a hand. As his primary caretaker and approaching 70 herself, she was wearing out. It wasn't a pretty sight. In the middle of the night I found him stark naked and standing over his bathroom sink, water running, his body rigid and paralyzed. The water had woken me up. He had no idea what was happening or how he'd gotten there, but I was able to get him back into bed.

That was about a month before Katrina. I had no reason to doubt my sister's assessment of the situation or the deep pain in her voice when she told me I should come as soon as I could. Kissing my partner Mack goodbye, I was on a plane the next day.

Getting into the area wasn't going to be easy. New Orleans International Airport was completely shut down except for emergency and military traffic. Same for roads in and out of the city. My parents had retired to the Mississippi Gulf Coast, to a spot pretty much in the direct path of Katrina. In the dead of night, having stayed up to watch incoming reports about the storm's predicted trajectory, they'd been able to get across New Orleans and make it all the way to west Louisiana, outside of Lake Charles, near the Texas border, where much of my mother's extended family still live. She's from tough Cajun stock, the French country people who, expelled from Canada once the British took over, settled in the swamps and watery byways of southwest Louisiana. It's remote country, inhospitable, hot and humid. Of the numerous small towns between Baton Rouge and Houston, Lake Charles is among the largest. After a flight from Cincinnati to Houston, and a puddle jumper into Lake Charles, my brother-in-law picked me up at the airport.

My mother and I slept in the waiting room that night, fitfully, having pulled together a few uncomfortable vinyl-covered chairs, surrounded by other evacuees waiting out news of their loved ones. In the morning, my mother, sister, and I stood around my father's bed, holding vigil over his pitifully wasted form, his breaths coming in slow but jagged. His face pinched in unconsciousness, he wouldn't ever open his eyes again. The nurses assured us it was only a matter of time.

My father died about ten hours after I arrived. His frail body and mind couldn't handle the stress of the evacuation. My mother was convinced the overtaxed hospital staff couldn't attend to him properly. He was a Katrina victim, one of many old, sick people who didn't survive the storm. He was fortunate to die in a bed, with family surrounding him.

Days later, we had his funeral and then waited for permission to get back into the affected areas to see what remained. For weeks, many folks were stuck in west Louisiana. My mother, sister, and brother-in-law, along with their three kids, stayed with an aunt and her adult children, many of whom lived in trailers or homes they'd built around their mother's trailer, off a small road that bore their family name. The water would often run brown for a bit when you turned on the tap. Eventually we learned that my sister's and mother's homes had negligible damage. An aunt, uncle, and their sons, though, had lost everything, flooded out of the city.

The people in the tour van want to see blight, which itself seems a bit creepy, a looking in on others who have suffered, a slight gawking at damages endured. There's not as much of it as there used to be. In 2006, I drove to the area with a photojournalist, Jon Hughes, to do a story about the devastation.[13] The storm surge had taken out nearly every building along Highway 90, the beachfront road on the Mississippi Gulf Coast. We saw miles and miles of abandoned homes that had sat under nine to twelve feet of water. Plenty of blight.

Nine years later, driving through the upper Ninth Ward, we see a destroyed home here and there, desolate with orange spray-painted X's still noting when the building had been inspected for remains, human and otherwise. Mostly we see newer homes now elevated, as much as ten feet off the ground, with carports holding empty the space for future floodwaters. Our guide points out how older homes had been lifted up, or just moved completely to somewhat higher ground. He talks about his home in Lakeview, flooded under eight feet of water, and the weeks and weeks of driving into the neighborhood with family to salvage, clean up, repair, and rebuild, returning to Baton Rouge after dark when the curfew came.

13 As always, thanks to Jon Hughes, not only for going on the original trip with me, but for allowing me to publish his photograph of me from that trip: Jon Hughes / http://photopresse.com/.

Habitat for Humanity and the city built the seventy-two homes of Musicians' Village, centered on the Ellis Marsalis Center for Music, providing music instruction for area youth. Brightly colored in oranges, purples, greens, a creole medley, they house local players, an attempt to preserve the city's jazz heritage. The wrecked and abandoned, next to the colorfully new, hopeful for the future.

Such contradictions are everywhere here. In a beautiful poem about the city, "before the storm: geographers in new orleans," Romanian-born American poet Andrei Codrescu writes about how his adopted city instills in its inhabitants a "knowledge of finitude that is intimately woven into our psyches / and that urges us to live intensely before the assured cataclysm."[14] Growing up, we always felt the "assured cataclysm," quite physically. Nearly every hurricane season we'd be packing the car to head west or north, fleeing a storm. We always knew that the city would eventually flood. The protecting levees were destined to fail. The waters that receded would surely rise again. New Orleans knows the cycles of life, celebrates them in its many festivals and its contradictions: its intense love of pleasure and its tolerance of corruption, its nurturing of the bon vivant and its deep racial segregations, its sexual openness and its intense homophobia.

The schools and churches that gave me a love of reading and music also taught me to hate myself. The relatives who fed me their delicious food withheld their love. Even after the storm, as we huddled in my aunt's trailer outside Lake Charles — my father dead, my mother and sister wondering if their homes still existed — one relative offered that Katrina was God's punishment on New Orleans for its sinful ways, and another complained to my aunt that Mack, my partner of 15 years, who had made it into the area for my father's funeral, shouldn't be allowed to stay in her trailer. We ate our boudin and shrimp creole, and I could only

14 Andrei Codrescu, *Jealous Witness* (Minneapolis: Coffee House Press, 2008).

thank the god who had struck my hometown that I'd escaped, however scarred.

One of New Orleans's nicknames is "the city that care forgot." I felt I knew those forgotten cares well. I still feel them, ghost bruises, creeping under my skin.

But in our tour guide's tone I hear a care that I'd not noticed before, or perhaps one that I didn't know how to hear. Maybe it's one that only Katrina and the failure of the levees could make audible for me. We stop at the 17th Street Canal, site of the most devastating levee breach of all. The guide's voice strains a bit. He's been talking for nearly three straight hours, but I sense something else happening. He's getting riled. He points out the massive construction — new walls, new pumps, new floodgates — but he's not proud. He wonders why all this wasn't here before. The van slows down so we can see the historical plaque marking the location of the breach. It's a typical brown piece of metal, and the guide reads the words with increasing emphasis, his voice cracking at the end:

> On August 29, 2005, a federal floodwall atop a levee on the 17th Street Canal, the largest and most important drainage canal for the city, gave way here causing flooding that killed hundreds. This breach was one of 50 ruptures in the federal Flood Protection System that occurred that day. In 2008, the US District Court placed responsibility for this floodwall's collapse squarely on the US Army Corps of Engineers; however, the agency is protected from financial liability in the Flood Control Act of 1928.

An "ooh" escapes from the back of the van, but we are otherwise silent until someone points to some of the houses around the levee, asking why anyone would want to live here again. The guide almost loses composure. Sitting in the front with him, I see his hands clench and unclench, the healthy pink of his face reddening a bit more. "This is the important part. We didn't ask to be flooded. Blame Uncle Sam."

I have to admit, I like his anger. I'm glad he's pissed. He should be. And he shouldn't tolerate the questioning from the back of the van, wondering why and what someone would choose: this is his home.

I am trying to understand how Katrina changed things for me. It's complicated. The storm, my father's death — a welter of ambivalent feelings and memories of my boyhood. Perhaps abandonment is a key here. I had abandoned New Orleans, feeling it had abandoned me, just as I had been emotionally abandoned by my father, and by a social world and Catholic doctrine that bullied and degraded me. I had decided to leave this place, that had left me first, and find family and home somewhere else.

In the aftermath of the storm, as I sat with my family, flooded out, my particular relationship to New Orleans was exposed, requiring an accounting of the bodies I'd left behind. And how could I think of those bodies, those intimacies bloating in my mind, and not think too on my own queerness, the queerness that drove me from my home? I remember my family, father, mother, sister, and me, sitting in a pizza parlor, a rare treat out. I must have been 11 or 12, and the Beatles' song "Got to Get You Back into My Life" comes on, and my father chuckles and quips about me: "That's what he thinks about me." He knew. He knew even then that he was a shitty dad, and I was growing up in a shitty place that would make me feel so outcast. As a child. A *child*. And after all these years, forty-odd years, that still stings, even as I've let so much of the hurt go. I realize the very first creep in my life was my father. But as I held my father in my arms while he died, I knew — and know to this day — that his lack of affection hadn't completely damaged my own ability to love, however creepily that love comes out at times.

Finally, nearly two weeks after the storm, my father's ashes packed in the car, we were able to get across the city back to our family houses — my mother's outside of Bay St. Louis in Mississippi, directly in the path of the storm, my sister's in Mandeville on the north shore of Lake Pontchartrain. Some shingles missing, some food wasted. Otherwise everything was all right.

I rode back with my cousin, just a couple of years older than me, someone I hadn't seen in two decades, possibly more. A devout man, he was generous of spirit, unlike many Christians I've known. He told me that he and his siblings had often wondered about me. I braced myself, but then he clarified. They'd wondered, but not because I'd been cast out: I was the one who had gotten away. They were intrigued, curious. They'd often imagined what it would be like to leave, though few of them ever did. I'd never even imagined such a perspective: that others, my cousins, could envy, even in a small way, my having moved on. That they identified in me a courage I couldn't acknowledge myself; I'd felt it, not as courage, but as the only way to survive.

A small thing? Maybe. But Katrina enabled me to hear it. It just feels a little creepy that it took such a catastrophe — such damage — to cut through the damage done to me.

There is part of me that thinks of Katrina all the time. Part of my fascination is its avoidability. Surely a Category 5 hurricane is a force to be reckoned with. But the damages exacerbated by human failing, by human negligence, demand an accounting. So too do the damages done *to* me, a young queer man, drowning in waves of homophobia. But I was beginning to feel lucky, sitting in that van, touring the damage, having survived. A creep, yes, but one who survived.

The tour over, I drive back to my mother's house. There are no pictures of Mack and me in my mother's home, although my sisters and their families have been on display for years. After setting my breakfast plate down in front of me, my mother heads to the bathroom, shutting the door behind her. I hear a tiny click as she locks the door. And I chuckle to myself. We are alone in the house. Whom does she think is going to walk in on her while she's urinating? It's hard for me not to hear that click as the reverberating sound of all of the silences between us — the lack of trust, the absence of intimacy, the truths untold. Am I a creep to her too, still, after all this time?

I'm always preparing myself for the worst. Stealing myself for the inevitable disappointment. Fortifying myself against the expected rejection. I don't wonder why anymore. And yet I've tried to be open to my mother's story, my father's, and others', such as Ackerley's and White's. And my own. I want to understand. I even, some days, want to forgive. Lidia Yuknavitch, that wonderfully creepy chronicler of her own damages, says late in her memoir, *The Chronology of Water*, "Maybe forgiveness is just that. The ability to admit someone else's story. To give it to them. To let it be enunciated in your presence. It's your job not to flinch."[15] Another way of not flinching is becoming aware of when we are creeped out — and not turning away. Obviously, you have to turn away from *some* creeps. But maybe not everyone. And if you've read this far, you may have flinched — you might still — but you haven't turned away. Not completely.

But I know it's hard. I told a good friend once about my father's work, about how he hated every day of his life what he did, and she expressed pity for him. But I don't want to have pity for him. I feel in myself an attempt to resist sympathy, and I recognize my creepiness in that withholding of pity, that turning him into an object, my refusing to see him as a damaged person himself — as the creep he was. At the same time, I can't deny that I also feel myself becoming dispassionate about former grievances, pain lessening with time. I'm worrying past worry a little more every

15 Lidia Yuknavitich, *The Chronology of Water* (Portland: Hawthorne, 2010), 306.

day, like a hole in a coat you no longer mind as you mindlessly finger it.

And then I remember one day, months after the storm, walking along the beach in Bay St. Louis, surveying the damage sustained. Someone had set up a Christmas tree on the beach amidst the debris. A bit creepy. But still hope in the middle of destruction.

Made in the USA
Lexington, KY
24 March 2018